THE GLOUCESTERSHIRE FLOODS 2007

THE EXPERIENCES OF GLOUCESTERSHIRE WI MEMBERS, THEIR FAMILIES AND FRIENDS

COMPILED BY
GILL THOMAS & SUE WILSON

SUTTON PUBLISHING

First published in the United Kingdom in 2007 by
Sutton Publishing, an imprint of NPI Media Group Limited
Cirencester Road · Chalford · Stroud · Gloucestershire · GL6 8PE

British Library Cataloguing in Publication Data
A catalogue record for this book is available from the British Library.

ISBN 978-0-7509-4946-0

Typeset in Photina 11/13pt.
Typesetting and origination by
Sutton Publishing.
Printed and bound in England.

contents

Mario Testino ©

foreword

I was delighted to be asked to write the foreword for this fund raising book – 'The Gloucestershire Floods 2007' – which describes so accurately the devastating impact of the flash floods on our community, as seen through the eyes of my fellow members of the WI.

What happened in July shocked us all. The flooding wreaked havoc in the towns and villages of Worcestershire and Gloucestershire. Lives were shattered, homes were wrecked, and livelihoods were threatened. It could not have been bleaker for those affected by this devastating natural disaster.

Yet when we visited Gloucestershire to see for ourselves how people were coping we were both warmed by the mood of hope, and the true British spirit. We saw this spirit in the men and women of our Emergency Services, who worked tirelessly to protect us and support us, and in the shattered communities where both old and young rallied together to help each other.

This book will become a permanent record of how the County of Gloucestershire coped so stoically under such difficult and hostile conditions with the floods of July 2007.

foreword

I am delighted to write this foreword and I feel sure that this book will provide many lasting memories for the people of the county of Gloucestershire who lived and worked throughout what was probably the single largest incident to affect peacetime Britain.

The events of July 2007 tested all our capabilities to manage such a challenging and many-faceted operation. It is testament to the tenacity and fortitude of good people within the organisations involved and the communities of Gloucestershire that we were able to progress the return to normality much quicker than was at first predicted.

Clearly the many threats we faced, particularly to our utility facilities such as the Castlemeads and Walham substations and the Mythe Treatment Works, were a major challenge to all the agencies involved. I am proud of the work carried out by all the organisations involved in addressing what was a major threat to many communities throughout the region. We must all make sure that everything possible is done to guard against a similar occurrence in the future.

Timothy Brain
Chief Constable of Gloucestershire

introduction

Dr Foster went to Gloucester
In a shower of rain,
He stepped in a puddle,
Right up to his middle,
And never went there again.

This well-known nursery rhyme is said to refer to a visit by Edward I to Gloucester when his horse got stuck in mud in a city street. How true, though, it might have been of people in so many parts of the county during the flooding which began on Friday 20 July 2007.

When five inches of rain fell in one day, widespread flash flooding occurred across Gloucestershire. Roads became rivers, water rushed off hillsides and trickling streams turned into raging torrents causing havoc as people struggled to reach their homes, some abandoning cars and wading through waist-high water, others stranded overnight on the M5 or having to make detours to spend the night with friends or in hotels and hastily set up rescue centres.

Many battled to save their houses from flooding; others were forced to just stand by helplessly as torrents of fast-moving water engulfed their belongings and their houses, while the emergency services and the RAF carried out many welcome rescues. Gold Command, headed by the Chief Constable, and made up of the main players in the emergency, was set up to take control of the situation.

As the water receded over the following days, the resulting rise in the river levels on the Severn and the Avon caused even more devastation. The town of Tewkesbury became an island, completely cut off by floodwater. On Sunday 22 July, the Mythe water treatment plant in the town was shut down after the works were flooded, leaving 150,000 homes without running water. It would be days before the floods receded enough for experts to get onto the site to see how much damage was done, but it was estimated it would be at least two weeks before supplies would return.

On Monday 23 July, electricity supplies to around 350,000 homes were endangered as the Castlemeads and Walham substations in Gloucester had been surrounded by water threatening to overwhelm them. The county held its breath that night as the next high tide on the Severn approached, and it was only the staunch efforts of the emergency services and the armed forces in holding the water at bay that ensured this disaster was narrowly averted.

By now the eyes of the national media had focused on the disaster and pictures of the county's plight were beamed around the world daily. HRH The Prince of Wales and HRH The Duchess of Cornwall made visits to Cheltenham and Tewkesbury, while HRH The Princess Royal visited Gloucester.

The water supply was not to return until Friday 3 August, and wasn't declared drinkable until three days later. In the meantime, Gloucestershire residents got used to not being able to flush the toilet or having a daily shower. Bottled water supplies were brought into Cheltenham Racecourse and distribution points were organised in supermarket car parks and village halls, with volunteers spending long hours lifting packs of bottles into car boots and making home deliveries to the elderly and vulnerable.

A new phenomenon arrived in Gloucestershire: the 'bowser'. Large, mostly blue, plastic tanks of all shapes could be seen trundling down the motorways and into the county from all over the country, along with tankers to fill them with drinking water – although this had to be boiled first. At first they were slow to appear, but then seemed to arrive mysteriously like aliens landing on street corners and in car parks – but some never seemed to arrive at all where they were needed. After a visit to the county by the Prime Minister, Gordon Brown, the Army were called in to help with the distribution of bowsers and bottled water, and the logistics improved.

A community spirit, lacking in many places in recent years, sprang up as neighbours helped one another to clear up after flooding or to collect water, and new friendships began as people filled their containers at bowsers. As the water supply gradually returned, letters were sent to every home explaining that it would not be fit for drinking for a few days.

Life gradually began to return to normal, but not for those living in the 4,000 homes that had been flooded. Belongings had to be thrown away, some of them holding precious memories that can never be replaced. Floors were taken up and plaster chipped away to allow the drying out process. Hundreds moved into caravans on their driveways where they will stay for many more months before their homes are habitable again. Five hundred businesses were affected by flooding; many of them will never get back on their feet. Fifty schools have been damaged and many of the county's roads are in need of repair. The cost of the clean up is expected to be over £50m.

There will be much discussion about whether building houses on flood plains was to blame for the extensive flooding and if this should be allowed to continue, or whether climate change causing freak weather conditions was the reason.

The summer of 2007 will go down in history as a time of crisis for Gloucestershire to which the county's residents responded with courage and determination. The stories and photographs on the following pages show how Gloucestershire WI members, their families and friends coped with the dramas that unfolded in front of them.

The Gloucestershire Flood Relief Fund was set up to aid those who suffered from the flooding and all proceeds from this book will go to the fund.

acknowledgements

Our grateful thanks go to HRH The Duchess of Cornwall and Gloucestershire's Chief Constable, Timothy Brain, for kindly writing forewords for this book; Matilda Pearce from Sutton Publishing, for her support and guidance and her enthusiasm for the book from the outset; all WI members, their families and friends, who reacted to the request for contributions for this project so speedily – whether they made it into the final edit or not. Without you all this book would not have been possible.

chapter one

GETTING HOME

Eunice Allen

Bredon WI

The BBC weather forecasters warned us we were in for heavy rain – we've heard that before! On the morning of Friday 20 July I drove to Bristol, returning at lunchtime for a funeral at Charlton Kings. As it was raining quite heavily and the traffic busy, I only just managed to get to the church on time. The funeral lasted well over an hour. When I parked, there was a bit of water underneath the car – but on my return to the car park the tyres were in water. I wanted to join the family for a drink at the Club, but decided to head home.

Traffic was virtually at a standstill in London Road in Charlton Kings, so I took a diversion, heading towards Prestbury. Approaching Bouncers Lane, I was driving through quite deep muddy water in places; it had come in torrents down Cleeve Hill. All roads to Bishop's Cleeve were closed. I eventually arrived at the outskirts of Tewkesbury, well on my way home and looking forward to a visit to the loo. The traffic was at a standstill and it soon became clear Tewkesbury was gridlocked. The M50 was flooded, I'd checked the M5 as I drove over it and that looked pretty chaotic – so I chose the A38.

Prestbury. (Frances Wilson)

I was slowly driving along when I heard on the radio that a rescue centre was being set up at the Tewkesbury Borough Council Offices. I thought about going to help – but decided I'd better try to get home. Suddenly, I felt a jolt. I'd been hit by the car behind. The driver had been cleaning his windscreen when his foot slipped off the clutch.

Eventually I got into Tewkesbury High Street and really needed the loo, so I stopped at a pub. On continuing my journey I decided to take a little deviation and eventually got onto Bredon Road. There was so much water but luckily my car just kept going. Between Tewkesbury and Bredon there were three areas with quite deep water, and driving through I could feel the force of the water. Most people were driving sensibly but some vehicles went too fast and sprayed everyone.

I drove into Bredon and wanted to take the road towards Eckington, but that was coned off, so I travelled to Westmancote and turned left past the cricket club. At the junction I stopped a driver and asked what the road was like. He took one look at the car and me and said it was impossible, but when I said I wasn't going too far, he said I might just make it. It was bad, but I did eventually arrive home safely.

Jenny Smith

Highnam WI

It was raining when I left home on Friday 20 July to visit an elderly relative near Upton-upon-Severn, and it continued all morning. My plan was to return to Gloucester via Tewkesbury.

The journey along the A38 towards Tewkesbury was soon cut short because, at the A38/M50/M5 interchange, the road to Tewkesbury was closed and the roundabout was already awash. I made a snap decision as I drove twice around the roundabout; Ross-on-Wye via the M50 was my only choice and my home was not so far from Newent. There was running water several inches deep on the M50, red in colour from the surrounding soil. In places the water got deeper and there was very little traffic in my direction. The northbound lanes were busy and eventually came to a standstill. The exit road to Ledbury was closed and I realised the Newent exit might be too. At one point I followed the car in front onto the central reservation to avoid the deepest flooding. I felt alone and terrified. It was a great relief when I found the Newent junction open.

I continued on toward Newent with much water in evidence; it was pouring out of the hedgerows across the road and a couple of the dips were beginning to fill up. Unfortunately, there was no way past the Travellers Rest pub at Malswick and a policeman directed me down into Newent. I was a bit dubious about this but I didn't want to leave my car on the side of the road like many had done, so I made for the highest spot in the car park at Budgens. The people at the supermarket were wonderful. I was panicking – my husband is disabled and would need me at home. I was given a hot drink and used the phone. I thought I was stranded for the night.

Sue, a very kind supervisor from Budgens, took me home with her. When Sue's husband came home he tried to take me home by a route that I could never trace again, and through water I would never have dared to cross. He got me to the other side of Churcham where the traffic came to a standstill. I decided to walk from there. The rain was still pouring down. At the same time a young woman with a little girl and a baby was abandoning her car. I carried the little girl through the water, which was up to our knees for most of the way to the Highnam turn off. Traffic was stationary, and complete chaos reigned. Some cars were attempting to travel into Gloucester on the wrong side of the carriageway and along the footpath. Many still had their engines running so there were exhaust fumes in the air and there was oil on the water from submerged vehicles. Opposite the entrance to Linton Farm was a cross current from a torrent of water rushing from the grounds of Highnam Court into the farmyard. Not a pleasant wade, but we made it. The young woman was determined to get into Gloucester so I left her. I feared for her safety more than once that night.

Cold, wet and hungry, I staggered into the house a quivering heap. A friend had fed my husband and the cat, and brought me some supper too. I was very glad to hear the next day that the young woman had arrived home safely and that I knew her mother. It's a small world!

Elizabeth James
The Shires WI

I caught the 2.50 p.m. bus to Newent. Slow traffic was passing single file through floods and although water came inside the bus, the lady driver was determined to get everyone home. When we reached Highleadon, some teenagers decided it would be quicker to walk. We later heard they had to swim through water by the Travellers Rest pub at Malswick. When we reached the pub, we saw drivers abandoning their cars and attempting to walk across the fields to Newent. Our driver rang the depot to check the height of the engine and then, with everyone sitting at the back on the highest section, she drove through and we were lucky the water didn't quite reach where we were sitting. We arrived to find the centre of Newent flooded, but at least my home was all right.

Heather Miller
Marle Hill WI

I drove from Derbyshire on Friday in torrential rain, arriving home at midday. My husband, Clark, was about to fetch our granddaughter, Beth, from Cleeve School. I joined him dressed in a T-shirt, light trousers and sandals. We broke

Floodwater rushing past a charity shop in the centre of Newent.
(Pat Muirhead)

Bishop's Cleeve.
(Yvonne Cole)

Waiting for the AA to arrive in Kayte Lane, Southam. (Heather Miller)

down in floodwater on Kayte Lane in Southam. I walked on to the school to meet Beth and we both got soaked to the skin.

Eventually we found Clark, who had managed to start the car. We stopped at Tesco and then set out to leave Bishop's Cleeve. We headed up to the motorway via the bypass. Again we met floodwater and broke down; this time it was terminal! We were close to a friend's home, so Beth and I went there and were treated to tea and chocolate biscuits, given warm towels and allowed to drip all over my friend's settee. A friend indeed!

Clark sent for the AA and joined us while he waited. As it got dark we returned to the car, as we didn't fancy the walk through the floods at night. At 11 p.m. the AA informed us they wouldn't be there until at least Saturday afternoon! Our daughter, Sarah, has friends who own a 4×4 Discovery, so they came to rescue us.

The AA, understandably rather busy, arrived at 2 p.m. on Monday to tow the car to the garage. It was 'beyond economic repair'.

Noelle Virtue

Senior Research & Campaigns Officer, NFWI

I'd travelled from London to attend a focus group meeting on packaging at the WI Federation office in Gloucester. At 2 p.m. I set off with Gill Thomas, the County Chairman, for Stroud station. The roads were flooded and manhole covers were gushing out water. We had to change route several times but eventually reached the station, only to find that trains to Swindon were suspended.

Gill drove me to her house where we found that trains were running between Swindon and London, so some builders working in Gill's house kindly offered me a lift to Swindon. Easier said than done! At one point we drove under a mile in an hour! Traffic around Swindon station was ridiculous, so I got out and walked.

People were milling around everywhere. After an hour wandering between the train and bus stations it looked hopeless. No trains were expected for the rest of the day and no buses for several hours, so I decided to find a room for the night, but soon found everywhere around Swindon was full. I imagined myself sleeping on the station with 200 other people.

Meanwhile, my partner, Simon, was calling everyone we knew to find me a bed. Hours later his mother decided to drive from Nailsworth to fetch me, but she had come about halfway when I was able to phone her to say a train was on its way. Everyone was ecstatic and half an hour later a train pulled in – Out of Service. Unbelievable! An hour later the London train did arrive and thankfully there were enough seats for everyone.

The train ride blew me away. We watched raging rivers flow below us, only to see street lamps in the middle of them. They were roads! Abandoned cars lay scattered in what appeared to be lakes. It is one thing to see photos in the media, but quite another to experience it first hand. I finally made it home around midnight to a warm, dry flat. There were many that night who didn't.

Mary Bartlett

Phoenix WI

We were returning from a holiday in Wales. By the time we got to Llandovery a gentle drizzle had became heavy rain. We stopped for lunch at Ross-on-Wye, hoping the now monsoon like rain would ease. It didn't, so we decided to head back to Cirencester via the M50 and M5.

Leaving Ross the traffic was fine but gradually slowed as puddles at the side of the road became larger. Eventually the hard shoulder became invisible as the water encroached on the inside lane. Traffic slowed right down to form a single column keeping as close to the centre of the motorway as possible. Two fire engines raced past on the flooded inside lane. Several lorries copied them, creating bow waves. Car drivers generally stayed safe in the outside lane. At each dip in the road there was a torrent of water rushing off the fields down the road to the bottom of the dip only to be met by another volume of raging water coming from the opposite side. Where they met, the road was totally flooded. From the passenger seat I could tell from the spray from vehicles ahead where the worst flooding occurred. We hoped and prayed it wouldn't get any deeper and that no one broke down. I remember glancing to one side expecting to see fields. There was nothing but brown water.

We eventually reached the M5 and joined three solid lines of slow traffic. People were driving very cautiously. There were large puddles of water but nothing like the floodwater on the M50. We felt rather smug that we had driven through worse and drove on at a snail's pace contemplating whether our house, by the side of a brook, would be safe. We counted down the junctions, finally coming off the motorway at junction 11a. Yippee! Good old A417 to Cirencester. Traffic was light. We sailed up Crickley Hill.

What a relief when we arrived home to find no floods. While making tea, we noticed some kind neighbours clearing debris from the drain in the road outside so that the surface water could drain into the stream. Strangely, the water level in the stream didn't rise until two days later, when the water meadow opposite flooded.

Adeline Rucklidge

Winchcombe WI

The Probus Lunch was at the Old Farmers Arms pub, near Bishop's Cleeve. We took the road through Gretton, but to our horror saw water bubbling up through the drains and considerable water on the road. Undeterred, we turned left towards Gotherington. Then a driver, turning back, informed us there was deep water round the corner, and it was impassable. Slightly perturbed, we went back to Gretton, down to the B4077 and then along the A435. With relief we saw the pub on our left, and parked.

We did notice water seeping in through the main door, but the staff were calm and served us a delicious meal. After the main course, they informed us the kitchen was 2ft under water! They would serve puddings but we might like to head home. That seemed sensible. I was put in a car with the Wadsworths.

Horror! The road that had before been difficult but passable was now a series of rivers running across the road. At the Teddington roundabout traffic was backed up on the Tewkesbury road, as traffic on and off the M5 was solid, so David took the B4077. It was scary, suddenly there were rivers rushing across the road with no indication of how deep they were. If you could see the white line it wasn't so bad, but otherwise it was guesswork. We went as far as the Gretton turn and stopped. The word was the road was

Fountains appearing in Back Lane, Winchcombe. (Alan Herod)

Car stranded in Greet Road, Winchcombe. (Alan Herod)

closed. The choices weren't great, either turn up to Gretton, we knew that was bad, or retrace our steps and turn towards Alstone and onto the Gotherington road. We were being told the road through Gretton Fields was impassable. Off we went back the way we had come! And the rain continued like a monsoon.

We noticed many cars parking at the Hobnails pub but continued on. The road through Alstone wasn't too deep, then onto the Gotherington road – an area deemed impassable earlier was the least of our worries. On into Gretton. There, the water bubbling up through the drains had caused dangerous areas where there was no idea of the state of the road underneath. There were also rivers rushing down roads from the hills to our right and across the main road.

It was difficult but David kept driving and eventually we were on higher ground, passing the 'Welcome to Winchcombe' sign with relief. Back Lane had its own water feature, a three-pronged fountain!

Some members were stranded in the Hobnails. Another car went to Alderton, and some checked into a B&B.

Floods under the railway bridge in Swindon Village, Cheltenham. (Sara Jefferies)

Flash flooding in Upton St Leonards. (Pam Tickner)

Annette Grafton

Bibury & Barnsley WI

Marooned in floods at Ampney St Mary, I sat in the car for five hours waiting for the AA. I accepted an invitation to shelter in the Red Lion pub, where the fire was lit, and was offered tea. I had no idea what to do. A couple, tired of sweeping out the floodwater from their home, had cycled to the pub to drown their sorrows. What surprise and delight when a neighbour from Bibury walked in and offered me a lift home. I abandoned my poor car. My relief on arriving home was short lived; my kitchen was flooded.

Traffic struggling to pass through flooding at Little Beckford. (Bryone Coupe)

Turning back near Tibberton proved tricky. (Phil Bevan)

Liz Daykin

WI County Secretary

It was Thursday 26 July before I got into WI House again following the downpour the previous Friday. I only went in for a couple of hours as there was no water, but it poured with rain again while I was there. My friend, Glenda, called to tell me the Highnam road was flooded again.

I looked out to the car park and saw my car surrounded with water, so I took a towel, rolled up my trousers, took off my shoes and waded out. Along the road, several places were flooded, the worst being the lane to my house. I looked at the water and thought 'Shall I or shan't I?' and decided to give it a go. Halfway in I thought, 'I shouldn't have done this,' but carried on slowly and reached the other side without stalling the engine. I was very relieved to get home.

chapter two

STRANDED

Valerie Martin

Gotherington, Woolstone & Oxenton WI

After an enjoyable week's holiday with my daughter and young grandchildren in Devon, I caught the train from Totnes, homeward bound for Cheltenham. The sun was shining and the coastal route beautiful. At Bristol the mood changed. Heavy rain. The train slowed and then stopped when we approached a tunnel. Two men walked through to make sure it was safe to proceed.

At Gloucester, the service was suspended. I rang my friend to tell her not to meet me at Cheltenham but she couldn't get out of Oxenton anyway because of flooding. Rainwater was flowing like a waterfall off the hills and the lanes at the backs of the houses were like rivers. I worried about my house being flooded.

Crowds alighted onto Gloucester station, no one knowing what to do. I felt alone and forlorn. Then I saw a 'crocodile' of elderly people, parents and children being ushered from the waiting room. I thought 'I'm old, I should follow!' So I did, through one door, along a corridor and out through another door into the street dragging my case in the pouring rain. We were directed to the Station Hotel, huddled like sardines, wondering what lay ahead, and knowing whatever happened could take a long time. The bar staff were rushed off their feet. We bought drinks and food. The Virgin train staff were excellent, giving the children hot chips. They kept us informed about weather conditions and arranged for ten coaches to come from Birmingham to pick us up. Trains were running normally further north.

By 6 p.m. there was good news and bad news. There was no chance of leaving Gloucester by road or rail. The coaches were stuck among gridlocked traffic on the motorway. All local hotels were fully booked and, as no taxis were available, we were to walk across to the GL1 Leisure Centre in Bruton Way, where we would be accommodated until the situation improved. I kept trying to phone my family, but the mobile networks were overloaded.

I had made friends with Miriam, who was en route from Cornwall to Chesterfield. We trudged through the rain and finally found GL1, a welcoming place. We had to register on arrival (and departure); over 500 people, some from the trains, others from flooded homes and abandoned cars. It was most efficiently organised and much appreciated. We were provided with tuna or cheese sandwiches, tea, coffee and squash.

There was a couple from California only four days into their visit to England. Another couple, who had emigrated to Australia thirty years ago, were back to visit relatives. Two young lads I sat opposite on the train were returning home to Hull after a Marine Commander Training Course in Devon. Two families going to meet other families for an annual college reunion. A single lady never parted from her dog wherever she went. A mature couple stranded after a wedding anniversary lunch. For all, a levelling experience.

Later that evening an announcement over the loudspeaker startled me. 'Would Valerie Martin please contact her daughters.' After several more attempts on my mobile I finally spoke to my family.

Cars stranded on Secunda Way, Hempsted. (Joan Heath)

Bedtime arrived. Part of the sports hall was sectioned off and lights turned down. Miriam and I, along with the other over sixties, parents and children, were provided with a yoga mat, pillow and duvet. Some slept soundly, others restlessly. There was a rustling sound like waves and I wondered if it was more rain, but later discovered it was foil sleeping bags. It felt like being in a very large hospital ward after a long night when you haven't slept too well, and then slowly realise where you are.

Early morning and people began emerging from their makeshift beds with an air of acceptance. Toilet facilities were excellent and breakfast was croissants or jam doughnuts. By 9 a.m. announcements were being made that those wishing to go north would have to travel by train to Bristol, then to London and up to Birmingham for a connection to northern services. So Miriam left.

Some time later it became clear the roads were accessible, so I left GL1 and caught the bus to Cheltenham. From there I walked towards the racecourse where a friend picked me up. It was a relief to be home again. I was lucky, the patio had turned into a pond but water didn't get into the house. Friends invited me to supper. I was glad of their company and enjoyed a welcome, hearty meal.

Pat Muirhead

Newent Lakeside WI

We have a brook running through Newent, which turned into a river and overflowed. Businesses in Broad Street were flooded and our main car park

Abandoned vehicles at Rudford. (Kate Ratcliffe)

turned into a second lake. Newent Lake burst its banks and several houses in Brookside and Peacock Gardens were flooded, as were many gardens.

A coach load of German students, stranded as there was no way out of our town, were put up in the Memorial Hall, and the local traders fed them. The only way into Gloucester for nearly a week was via the M50 and the M5.

Shirley Baddeley
Bredon WI

We left our son's home in Beaconsfield at 10.45 a.m. on Friday 20 July, aware that the weather nearer home wasn't very good. The M40 was flooded across both carriageways in places and the spray was dreadful. Never mind, we arrived at the supermarket in Evesham to shop for necessities before reaching home.

We continued our journey but found to our dismay that our usual road to Pershore was closed. After asking a policewoman whether we could get down the next road, we spent two hours travelling through Evesham, only to find that the road had just closed. We eventually made it to the M42 and on to the M5,

Going under in the lane to Deerhurst. (Tony Price)

No riding today! Gabb Lane in Apperley.
(Rose Williams)

but the motorway was very slow moving. Finally we turned off onto another road to Pershore, only to be caught between two flooded areas. After sitting in the car for what seemed like hours (but was actually only two) we realised that, if we turned round, we might get back the way we'd come. This we did and once more found ourselves on the M5, but this time the traffic was stationary. We followed some other motorists down the hard shoulder and into Strensham Services. It was chaos – people were double parking and the cafeteria was out of food. There were, however, loos and we had a cup of tea. We then settled down for a night in the car, which was not very comfortable but preferable to sleeping on the cafeteria floor, which many did.

At 6.30 a.m. on Saturday morning the motorway was slowly moving again. It was 10.45 a.m. (24 hours after leaving Beaconsfield) when we parked about 200yd from home. Good, we thought, we can walk from here – wrong – the house was surrounded by 5ft of water and the RNLI were rescuing people from their homes by inshore lifeboat.

We went to stay with our son in Bolton. We only had the clothes we stood up in, which we'd been wearing for two days. Thank goodness for M&S and a nice hot shower! We couldn't return home until Tuesday 24 July, but were lucky as our living quarters are over the garage and the only things destroyed were in the garage – including a 4-wheel drive vehicle!

June Satterthwaite

Ebrington WI

Two of our members had to be resourceful in finding their way home. One was in Cheltenham on Friday afternoon. She hadn't driven far before realising she wasn't going to be able to leave the town, so she returned to the Park and Ride and took a bus back into town where she went in search of a B&B, finally getting home around 11.30 a.m. on Saturday morning.

The other member had just returned from Tenerife with her daughter. They had driven as far as Halford when they found they couldn't cross the River Stour because the bridge was severely damaged. They tried various ways of reaching their home in Blockley, but failed. On the outskirts of Stratford, the police advised them to stop trying and find some accommodation. They spent the night in a four-poster bed in the Victoria Hotel, arriving home after further diversions well into Saturday.

Liz Hope

Fairford WI

Water ran off the main USAF runway into Whelford near us. Our daughter-in-law, Lucy, got caught there and her car is now a write-off – the water was so deep. Her sister, Rachael, had to be rescued and taken home to Hatherop, while her brother Mark's car was abandoned, and wrecked, near Evesham. My nephew's wife and small daughter were stranded in their car by the new Lechlade roundabout for five and a half hours – they were eventually rescued by a fire engine.

Janet Waters

Bishop's Cleeve WI & The Shires WI

Working at Shire Hall, I normally fight for a parking pass, so I felt lucky to have one on Friday 20 July. How wrong could I be! A message at 2.12 p.m. for all non-essential staff to leave added that part of Quayside car park was flooded. Traffic was gridlocked and the lower end of Quay Street was under water. Even worse, my small hatchback sat forlornly in several inches of water. Nothing for it but to wade through, it was well over the top of my shoes.

People were panicking and jostling inch by inch to leave the car park, and the traffic on the roads was barely moving. I crawled through the city centre towards Cheltenham via London Road and Cheltenham Road. An hour later I reached Elmbridge Court and, as the Golden Valley seemed to be at a standstill, I decided to go through Churchdown.

In first gear, I edged past the garage and the garden centre until I met my first flood, just before Dowty's. I was frightened, but wanted to get home to my son in Bishop's Cleeve, so drove carefully through. Then traffic stopped; a huge flood covered the road and even the number 94 bus had decided against attempting it. Horrified, I watched as some cars stalled. There was a collection of them in Dowty's entrance. I turned back and crawled very slowly to the Down Hatherley turning where I met a large 4×4. The driver told me not to go that way. I was really scared now but had to return to Churchdown and face the flood there again, just managing to get through. The rain was unrelenting and my petrol was running low. The petrol station was closed and the police had closed the road to Elmbridge Court roundabout, so I had to turn back again.

I vaguely remembered a back road through Churchdown to Shurdington so tried that. At Shurdington I hit traffic again and knew I would never make it home, so headed for a friend's house in Leckhampton. Thankfully they were home so I stayed the night. While there I discovered that the roads to Bishop's Cleeve were impassable from early afternoon, so I never had a chance of getting home.

There was a light drizzle when I started out at 8 a.m. the next morning. From the racecourse onwards a surreal scene greeted me of cars, vans and lorries abandoned at all angles. A flood by Smiths was still so deep cars weren't attempting it, so I tried another route. Kayte Lane was flooded but passable; there was an abandoned car in the ditch. I arrived home eighteen hours after leaving work, totally drained from my experience.

Marian Enstone

Bredon WI

A friend set out at lunchtime for an appointment at Cheltenham General Hospital, and eventually arrived home the following morning! For hours she drove around looking for a safe route back to Tewkesbury. Eventually, as darkness threatened, and very distressed, she found shelter (and a loo!) in a little village near Newent. Although there were no guest rooms at the pub, the landlady provided pillows and a blanket and a couple of armchairs in the bar as a makeshift bed.

Gander Lane in Tewkesbury became impassable.
(Matilda Pearce)

The road disappeared at the Red Lion, Wainlode. (Jennie Moss)

Peter Stevens, husband of Erica Stevens

Lechlade WI

We'd been to Scarborough for a few days and had left mid-morning. On reaching Leicester I remarked that there could be rain in the distance. As we left the M1 and joined the M69 it started, becoming heavier and heavier.

Our problems started along the A429 towards Moreton-in-Marsh where we joined a long traffic jam. Water was flooding off the fields across the road, leaving just the centre open. We then came to a roundabout with traffic travelling the wrong way round it. Some cars had attempted to travel the correct way round, only to become submerged up to their windscreens. We got through with water up to our doorsills, thinking our troubles were over.

Further on, more traffic jams. Then a large lorry came along the road with the driver hanging out of his window warning other drivers, 'I've been to Moreton and had to turn back – you have no chance'. We decided to go back to the first turning and try to make our way across country and through Chipping Campden.

We went through small hamlets and along country roads, and now the call of nature was urgent. There weren't any cars around so we looked for a place to relieve ourselves, but at every gateway the water was deep and we would have been up to our ankles in mud. Finally we came across a place where the road was higher than the field entrance and the tarmac sloped down into the gateway, which meant it wasn't flooded. I was okay, but my wife had to hold onto the car door handle because of the slope with me pushing the door closed and holding up the umbrella with my other hand. We had just regained our composure when three cars and a jogger out for a run in the rain came along!

Suddenly a warning came over the car radio that Chipping Campden was impassable, so where to next? We thought we'd try Broadway, so off we went, and on reaching the A44 found the road to Stow-on-the-Wold was moving. We carried on with optimism. Then we heard that the Burford to Lechlade road was closed. We weren't going to get home and needed somewhere to spend the night.

We had spotted a B&B in Stow and decided to try there. Imagine our surprise when a Danish gentleman opened the door, explaining that the landlady was travelling to Cheltenham to collect her mother but wasn't sure if they would get back, so she was asking guests to look after the house. Luckily, he had just taken

Roads became impassable for those trying to head for home in Lechlade. (Erica Stevens)

a call from a guest, cancelling their room. It wasn't grand but had a four-poster bed, which was about 4ft 6in off the ground with a stool at each side to climb up.

The evening was spent with our four new Danish friends who invited us to have dinner in a hotel nearby. It seemed everyone there was stranded too. We later returned to our B&B, where I manned the door and took phone calls until 11.30 p.m.

Next morning, after breakfast, we discussed with our Danish friends where they should head for the next stage of their English holiday, took photos and then exchanged e-mail addresses, before we all set off on our respective ways.

Betty
Tibberton & Taynton WI

On Friday afternoon I set off from Tibberton to Cheltenham with my aunt, aged 93. We left for home via the A40 at around 3.30 p.m. – water all the way, finally reaching the safety of Tesco on St Oswald's Road in Gloucester at around 10 p.m.! We spent the night in the restaurant despite it being closed. The management were very kind, providing hot drinks, banana sandwiches and a copy of *The Times* to read.

Tibberton – almost at its deepest. (Kate Ratcliffe)

Gaynor Williams
Lechlade WI

We left Betws-y-coed at 3 p.m. Problems began soon after leaving the A5 at Shrewsbury. Conditions gradually worsened with a series of diversions and then driving through fast flowing floodwater across Shropshire and Worcestershire. Unsuccessful in finding a hotel for the night, we headed down the M5 towards Gloucestershire. After a short distance, we decided to follow our planned route to Evesham, but after half a mile of deep floodwater we had to retrace our route to the M5, which we thought was the safest place to be, realising there was water on every road around us.

Later, local radio informed us the M5 was closed near Tewkesbury, but we reached the slip road to Strensham Services where we came to a halt. Emergency vehicles, some towing inflatable boats, struggled through the traffic.

After several hours, we walked to the services to find hot drinks and toilets. Back in the car again, traffic started moving but only went a few hundred metres before stopping again, this time for the night. We had the remains of our holiday food and some water and managed to doze for a while.

At 5.30 a.m. we began to move again and were amazed at all the floodwater around Tewkesbury, the devastation and the abandoned vehicles. We drove through a dazed Cheltenham and headed for the high ground of the A40. All went well until we reached Burford and found the road to Lechlade was barred. As we had a 4×4 car we decided to try and get through. Luckily the water had subsided and we arrived home tired and relieved. We gave the car a pat on the bonnet.

Kind neighbours had kept a watch on our house. Floodwater had only just entered our garage and all was well. Some of them weren't so lucky. Over the next few days we had to restrict our flushing and bathing as our sewers were backing up and several manholes were bubbling in the streets. The boats on the Thames looked surreal with their mooring ropes fastened to invisible banks.

Mary
Tibberton & Taynton WI

After leaving work in Newent, I visited my mother (91) who was upstairs without electricity, her ground floor being flooded. I spent the night with her, concerned, however, about my partner, Tom, and unable to contact him with no mobile phone. By shouting across to a neighbour's house, I was able to contact fellow WI member, Di, in Tibberton. She visited Tom, who is partially sighted, taking him tea and a sandwich and reassuring him.

Angela Keen
Box WI

My daughter, Philippa, lives in Tewkesbury next to the lock and experienced quite an adventure! She left home as usual on the morning of Friday 20 July to teach at a school in Pershore. By the end of the day there just wasn't any way she could get home. Eighteen staff stayed at a colleague's house in Evesham overnight while others slept in the school. It was ten days before she got back into her flat, and that was using waders. Apparently the water was roaring past the house, and the lock keeper and remaining boaters had to be rescued by firemen. Since the house is built on stilts, the water level fell just short of the front door. Sadly the vegetable garden perished – for the second time this summer!

Stella Learwood
Norton WI

On Friday 20 July the road from Norton to Tewkesbury and Gloucester was impassable. The following day the water had started to recede and one could travel with caution.

Negotiating floods on the Tewkesbury Road in Gloucester. (Stella Learwood)

The A38 from Twigworth Garage (top left) to Longford (top right), with the land out of Sandhurst (bottom). (Jennie Moss)

The A38 at Priors Norton. (Kevin Cahill)

On Sunday, my husband Bob and I decided to drive to Tesco by the old cattle market to get his *Sunday Telegraph* and do some shopping. We were there about an hour. Heading home, we found the road by Plock Court ankle deep in water. We gingerly drove through to find the police had cordoned off the Tewkesbury road at the Longford roundabout. The road was impassable. We only live three miles up the road, but they were adamant we wouldn't get through. Hatherley Brook had burst its banks. We decided to risk it and they lifted the barrier, but after a few yards several ladies came running through the floodwaters imploring us to stop as our wake would send a huge wash into their homes. We turned round and drove back to Tesco, where they kindly agreed to keep our perishable shopping in their chiller store.

Paddling past the Winfield Hospital, we repaired to the Longford Inn and had a bite to eat. I telephoned my daughter, who said Newnham was fine and we could stay with them there until things got better. On Tuesday my son-in-law went to work at GCHQ so we joined him to see what conditions were like at Norton. We had to drive to Chepstow and over the Severn Bridge, up the M5 to Cheltenham, then up Down Hatherley Lane. We hadn't been flooded, but had no tap water so we returned to Newnham for another few days.

Tesco were very good. During the flood their chiller lost electricity and our goods were thrown away, but as we had the receipt, they replaced everything.

Irene Jones

Horsbere WI

The disastrous torrential rain and subsequent flooding in and around Gloucester left me stranded in Birmingham, where I'd gone to visit my elderly sister before leaving for a holiday in Canada.

On hearing the devastating news of the extensive flooding around the Longlevens area where I live I was very anxious to return home, but as both the M5 and the rail links to the West Country had been closed it was impossible to get home. On hearing further news that the Gloucester area had lost both electric power and drinking water I was easily persuaded to remain in Birmingham.

My home in Longlevens was in one of the areas badly hit by flooding, as the Horsbere Brook, which runs along the bottom of my road, had burst its banks. Fortunately, I was able to contact a neighbour by telephone and be assured that although floodwater had entered the houses further down the road, it hadn't reached mine. I was, however, extremely anxious to return home as soon as possible as I was due to leave for Canada the following weekend. On Tuesday 23 July I managed to book a seat on a National Express coach for Cheltenham, packed my suitcase with bottles of drinking water –

along with a few candles and matches – and carried my personal belongings in a carrier bag.

The situation at home looked extremely dire with the evidence of floodwater, effluent and debris around the houses at the bottom of my road. Stories soon reached me of the dreadful conditions in other parts of Longlevens, and of people having to leave their homes and take refuge with relatives and friends, not knowing when or if they would be able to return.

I did leave for Vancouver as planned and my family in Canada were eager to hear my first-hand experiences of the floods, which had been widely shown on television there, and as there had been no water available for baths or showers at home, I was grateful for a long, hot, perfumed soak in their beautiful bath.

chapter three

FLOODED

Jan Mundy

Tirley WI

At 1.10 p.m. I was busy in my office in Tewkesbury, heavy rain pounding against the window, when the phone rang, informing me our street in Tirley was about to flood.

My husband, Hugh, left immediately and I followed fifteen minutes later. Hugh arrived home around 2 p.m. The floodwater was halfway up the drive, so he placed a submergible pump in the porch with a board and sandbags in front to pump water away from the front door – this worked well until the water came in from the back of the house and out through the letterbox behind him. He gave up and took a few items upstairs and put furniture on blocks.

On leaving the office I tried our normal route home, but the floods were too high near Apperley so I tried the Mythe route instead. At the traffic lights by Morrisons supermarket there were long delays due to the volume of traffic and the traffic lights not working. Half a mile from home, vehicles had been abandoned by a stretch of high water. A vehicle passed me and went through in the centre of the road, so I followed and then parked at the village hall.

An aerial view of the 'Isle of Tewkesbury'. (Jennie Moss)

I walked towards our house. The road was flooded and our caravan was floating in the drive. We obviously couldn't go home, so Hugh and I went to my sister-in-law Hilary's house further up the road. No one was in, but we were sure they would be soon as their donkeys, alpacas and dogs would need feeding, so we waited in the car. After an hour we drove back to the village hall.

Our clothes were very wet and we were cold and suffering from shock. We were sitting with the heater running, trying to keep warm, when Keith and Chris, walking their dogs, tapped on the window. They took us home for a shower and gave us dry clothes and a meal. When we'd recuperated we talked about another neighbour, Simon, who wasn't home but had a dog, which was usually left outside.

We ventured out again and through our paddock to the back of our house. We could see our new fridge through the kitchen window floating on its back in the water. Hugh struggled inside and waded through the 4ft deep water to check on our cat. He'd been sensible and gone upstairs, and was very pleased to see him. Hugh packed some clothes in a case, found his sister's spare key and placed some water and food upstairs for the cat until we could come back to rescue him properly.

Hugh, Chris and Keith all had wellingtons (I was in Chris's spare trainers) so they waded into the water to find Simon's dog. Water rushing across the road towards the fields opposite nearly knocked them off their feet at times. They held onto each other and made it safely back. Chris and Keith returned home and we went to Hilary's and fed the animals, then cleaned ourselves up and made tea.

Hilary rang at around 9.30 p.m. They had been to Charlton Kings and were trying to get back, but due to the problems with the motorway were making slow progress. By 11.15 p.m. they'd only gone another quarter of a mile and told us not to wait up. We went to bed but couldn't sleep. When they got home at 3 a.m. the flooding in our street had gone.

In the morning, we all went to our house to survey the damage and were overwhelmed with our neighbours' generosity; many helped us sweep the mud out, clear the debris and remove all the damaged furniture. Once our house was clear they went onto the next and continued doing this for the remainder of that day – they were heroes!

We took our cat back to Hilary's and he stayed in the library, but after a week his coat lost condition and we were worried about him.

On Friday 27 July we went to Oxford to stay with friends for the weekend. This was just the break we needed and the first thing we did was to have a shower. I couldn't stop washing my hair; I must have used a quarter of a bottle of shampoo!

We stayed at Hilary's until 8 August and then decided to take the cat back home. We're negotiating with the insurance company and cleaning up our home, and our cat is now very happy with his black coat in top condition again.

Liz Hope
Fairford WI

The River Colne broke its banks and cut Fairford off – the main A417 was closed for a week. In over seventy years my husband had never seen the river so high or the main road so badly flooded. The local restaurant 'Allium' put a table up in the Market Square to give away all its perishables (lettuce, cucumbers etc.), as they too were badly flooded.

June Satterthwaite
Ebrington WI

Ebrington was lucky but we had five neighbouring properties severely affected, caused mainly by a blocked culvert intended to divert surface water from fields. Chipping Campden was very seriously affected.

Maureen Kerry
Leonard Stanley WI

My daughters both live in Tuffley. They each have two children and were without running water for nine days and without electricity for two. One of my daughters, who lives in Bodiam Avenue, has a stream at the bottom of her garden, which rose within inches of flooding her home. Others in the same avenue were not so fortunate.

The River Colne overflowed causing flooding at the bottom of the High Street in Fairford.
(Carole Doherty)

Bryone Coupe

Beckford WI

With water surrounding our home like a moat, we watched it rising, wondering whether it would rise to claim our house, as it had others in Little Beckford.

Earlier we'd had to abort a trip to our granddaughter's birthday party in Wiltshire. Instead, my husband spent a couple of hours knee-deep in water with a neighbour directing traffic on the A46. In the end they gave up, as inconsiderate drivers ignored their advice and barged through, unaware of the damage they were causing to properties at the entrance to the village. The end result was a mass of abandoned cars.

Keeping an eye on the water level rising at the back of our home, we forgot that the dining room is six inches lower than the rest of the house, and by chance discovered water coming up through the floor and through the walls and spreading across the carpet. We got the furniture onto bricks and everything movable upstairs, and then watched, helpless.

This brand new caravan in Tuffley, Gloucester, was totally destroyed. (Pat Watts)

A friend had been trying for several hours to get back to Winchcombe from Cheltenham. Parking her car in a farmer's gateway, she walked knee-deep in water a quarter of a mile to us and we gave her hot food and drinks and a bed for the night.

The next day the flooding had gone, but what a mess! As we and our neighbours got rid of sodden carpets and moved damaged furniture into gardens, all we could do was help each other with the cleaning and provide meals where needed.

The following week I had an operation and, as our water supplies were unaffected, in exchange for providing showers, water and doing washing for friends and family, I received meals. Everyone helped each other in so many ways.

Diana Collins

Bredon WI

I was in my living room. It was raining heavily and my lawn became a lake. I brought my conservatory furniture inside. Before too long the patio filled with water and all my pot plants floated about. The water came into the house, flooding the ground floor – eight inches of water. I opened the front door and the water went through like a river.

My wonderful neighbours took most of my furniture upstairs and helped clear the water. It was lucky I was home as I had taken a friend to Cheltenham General Hospital that morning and was going to spend the weekend with my son.

Marion Gilliland

Kemble & Ewen WI

The River Thames flows through Kemble and Ewen and the water table rose so suddenly that River Cottage, close to the river between the two villages, had rainwater and sewage erupting in its garage. A couple of miles across the fields,

The source of the Thames is a small spring marked by a stone plaque. The fields are normally dry. (Marion Gilliland)

the Thames source, which in summer is usually dry on the surface, was bubbling vigorously and inundating fields to the west, beyond the source itself: a phenomenon not known for at least a generation.

Andree Boddington

Lechlade WI

For the first time the River Thames covered two meadows, a field of barley, and one of 'short-stalked' wheat – a perfect crop ready to harvest with water up to the 'ears': in all covering four fifths of a mile. Fortunately, here the ground begins to rise and it drained quickly. It's now been harvested and I think the crop was saved.

Velma Sutton

Apperley & Deerhurst WI

We arrived for a long weekend in Sherwood Forest after a journey through floods and heavy traffic. Our house-sitter, Pam, called to say she was using the contents of the airing cupboard to stem the flow of water cascading down the steps and in through our front door, but everything was under control!

Saturday dawned, still wet, and Pam kept us informed about the level of the River Severn, two fields away. When it overflows our field floods but the cottage is safe on a high bank.

That night the water level peaked, and our neighbour was confident he could keep the river at bay with pumps. The water rose so fast though that he couldn't and the next morning we received some alarming calls: 'The patio's flooded!' and 'The water's one brick below the French doors!' then 'Water's creeping into the kitchen', and finally 'Things are dire. The whole ground floor is under water!' We travelled home, hampered by road closures, traffic and heavy rain, feeling gloomy.

Another call made me feel easier; 'The donkeys are in the paddock, with the offer of a neighbour's field if things get desperate, the cats are in the guest bedroom, the dogs have been taken in by friends and the tortoise is in the bath out of harm's way!'

When I saw the house my heart sank. Toffee-coloured water was swirling around inside. Then a surprise. Friends had moved everything they could. Furniture had been raised on bricks and everything else ferried upstairs. The kitchen was more depressing. One step below the rest of the cottage, it had flooded first. The antique pine dresser and kitchen table were a write-off, and over a foot of foul-smelling water was in the cupboards. The new log burner had water up to the door handle.

The patio and front garden, with floodwater receding. (Velma Sutton)

We were hungry so we headed to Gupshill Manor and were astounded to see the car park full of emergency vehicles. A woman came out and shook her head at me. I said 'Oh no! Don't tell me you're not doing food! We haven't eaten all day and our house is flooded.' She replied 'Yes I know. You're staying with us.' That's how we met Sue and Ginger from the next cottage up the hill. They'd only just moved in. We hadn't met before but got on as if we'd known each other for years.

Gwen Booth (aged 90+)

Moreton-in-Marsh WI

Water rose from a nearby brook, gushing through the front of the house and then the garden room at the back. Amanda, my daughter from California, was staying and helped move furniture. Neighbours supplied pillowcases hastily filled with sand to barricade doors. Carpets were lifted by the water and I was carried across the car park to a neighbour's house for the night. Building blocks borrowed from nearby were used to lift furniture up. Since then I have stayed in a holiday cottage, then with some kind church friends, and later with other neighbours, and tremendous support has been received from the insurance company.

Bourton-on-the-Water, or, as it became known, 'Bourton-in-the-Water'. The green in the High Street turned into a lake. (Carole Bates)

Margaret Hunter

Naunton WI

The Windrush burst its banks and water from the hills around added to the torrent of water running down the road through Naunton. The speed of the water rising took many by surprise. Our secretary, Audrey, was badly flooded and is now in an apartment in Broadway while her cottage is made good. Also among those affected were four new families to Naunton who had only moved in three months prior to the flooding.

Vera Topham

Norton WI

We've lived on top of the hill at Priors Norton for fifty years. Our back garden overlooks meadows towards the Severn and the Malvern Hills. We've never seen

Looking upriver towards Tewkesbury, with Sandhurst Hill in the middle. (Jennie Moss)

them flooded in summer before. The hay has usually been cut and stored by now, but this year's crop is ruined. Thankfully, the sun came out, dried everything and took away the unpleasant smell. What will happen to them now? We must wait and see.

Barbara Raven

Priors Park WI

Our cottages in Barton Road are over 160 years old and just 10ft from the main road to the M5 and Ashchurch. There are no records of them flooding before. As rain poured down, I watched the water creep along the road from Morrisons supermarket. The drain outside was full of water, the kerbside gutters slowly filled, for the water, like me, had nowhere else to go.

Water from Oldfield Estate opposite scudded around the corner into our road and towards Morrisons – closing that way out of Tewkesbury. As the water speed increased I rolled up kitchen mats and dogs' mats, put them into bin bags and placed them across the porch. Traffic was still using the Oldfield turn. The water, now 3ft into our tiny front garden, was being sent halfway up our front door by passing traffic. I started putting things up onto stools. By morning the water was about eight inches deep in the house. The outbuilding at the back is lower, so it was deeper there. I have arthritis so my husband had to bail out what water he could.

Furniture, kitchen and electrical equipment are all ruined; also our books, including my grandmother's family Bible. Floors, skirting boards and walls will all need to be replaced or repaired. And the final straw – my mobility scooter keeps shorting out and cannot be used!

Vi Banks

Longlevens WI

The babbling brook became a torrent and by late afternoon we had a river running down our little road. The water started coming into our garden at the back, the patio was flooded. It was quite tense and stressful wondering whether or not we would be flooded. We were relieved to see the water gradually receding at the back, but the river in the road at the front of the house was getting deeper and deeper. It seemed to bring adults and children with gay umbrellas. They were all paddling and laughing and enjoying the river. However, water finds its own level and I knew the water would make its way to the Severn.

Elizabeth Harvey

Priors Park WI

I didn't go out again on Friday 20 July after the Country Market, but I did move my wellingtons into the back porch! I listened to BBC local radio reporting the escalating problems and later realised there was no traffic on the main road. I was surprised at 10 p.m. when friends in Barton Road phoned asking if I was alright. They had seen floodwater at the entrance to our close.

At about 2.15 a.m. I heard knocking on the front door and realised people were talking outside. I got up and looked through the back window. Lights were on in houses and people were moving cars further up the close. I could see streetlights reflected in the shallow water on the road. By 3 a.m. water levels seemed lower so I went upstairs and fell asleep, despite helicopters zooming above the rooftop and the sirens of emergency vehicles.

The playing fields at Plock Court. (Pauline Hill)

Church Street in the centre of Tewkesbury. (Elizabeth Harvey)

Everyone pitched in to fill DIY sandbags in Wynards Close. (M. Greenland)

View over the Mythe water treatment plant towards Tewkesbury Abbey. (Margaret Bailey)

When I woke again at about 7 a.m. I was relieved to find my house wasn't flooded, though there had been an inch of water in the garage. So it was on with the wellies, taking photographs and discussing events with neighbours; there was no water in adjacent houses but others fifty yards away were flooded, as were many on Barton Road, including my concerned friends. As I brushed water from the garage, helicopters were still busy overhead. Radio broadcasts confirmed Tewkesbury was now an island, cut off by the floodwaters.

Sunday the 22nd was bright, sunny and warm. I waded out from the close for an early walk around town, taking photographs. It was only the second time I'd seen floodwater in Church Street between the Crescent and the Hop Pole.

We seemed to have our own lake in the centre of the close. A council truck drove in and delivered sandbags and in the afternoon sand was tipped on the far side of the lake. Everyone sprang into action filling sandbags, while wheelbarrows, a sack truck and even empty wheelie bins were commandeered to move sand and sandbags through the lake to protect doors etc. Elderly folk and those at work had bags placed around their doors. This caring attitude continued, and included shopping and delivering bottled water.

The Mythe Waterworks flooded and we were told that in a day or so we would lose our water supplies, but that night I needed a hot bath to ease my aching muscles, while there was still water in the tap!

On Tuesday the floods disappeared from the Link Road (between Oldfield and Priors Park), which meant we could reach the A38 south of Tewkesbury.

Joan Davis

Priors Park WI

I live on a hill in Priors Park. My garden slopes down towards the house so rainwater came in through the back door, where I stood, with a bucket and mop, feeling like King Canute managing to keep the waves at bay.

My son and daughter kept me supplied with water from bowsers and bottled water and did my shopping. We were without power for two days so lived mainly on salads and made tea with a camping stove. I washed my 'smalls' using water from the water butt.

I needed to renew a prescription but the surgery in Tewkesbury was under water so I had to see an emergency doctor at the Borough Council Offices. The dispenser couldn't get into Tewkesbury so a friend took me to a Boots chemist near Cheltenham. We needed to show identification before the police would allow us back into Priors Park.

The centre of Tewkesbury, with the flour mill (bottom right). (Jennie Moss)

Margaret Sollars

Prior Park WI

It was the roar of a helicopter that dragged the residents of Webber House in Tewkesbury out of their sleep as dawn broke on Saturday 21 July. It hung there, like a huge angry wasp, and then wheeled away into the slowly brightening sky. As the light grew stronger, we saw the flood. A great brown sea stretched from the bottom of our garden over the Vineyards, past the Abbey and into the town centre.

Later, the silence on the A38 was unnerving. The police were turning back traffic further up the hill – though many drivers pulled in and walked to the water's edge, staring in disbelief. As the morning wore on, more sightseers came down the hill – families with children in wellies – teenagers riding bikes into the water – quickly frightened off by the rapidly increasing depth!

The media with their white vans, equipment and miles of cable were there in full force. They'd set up a small marquee with chairs and a table and a crate of

National and local press arrived in force. Jon Snow reported from Tewkesbury for Channel 4.
(Matilda Pearce)

bottles on the grass verge. But what could we do but stand staring over the brown water past the roofs of submerged cars in the Gloucester Road car park to the first little houses and shops and cafés along Church Street, all with water lapping their window sills?

Esme Anderson

The Village, Charlton Kings WI

On Sunday 24 June the roar of the usually docile River Chelt was the first sign that all was not well. The noise was deafening and quite frightening. We had expected a rise in the water level as there had been torrential rain in previous weeks.

When my partner Richard tried to leave for work the following morning the river covered the bridge between our close and the road, cutting us off. We have one house between us and the river (No. 1). We're several feet higher than them and we watched with horror as the water rose over their garden, up over the wheels of the car in the driveway and entered the house. We saw it swishing around in their conservatory. Fencing panels at the back of No. 1 were swept into the river, adding to the debris piling up along the bridge railings, causing water to come up our drive. Unfortunately, our neighbours were away for a few days.

Meanwhile, the water was rising at the side of our garage and making inroads across our back garden. We went into 'siege mode'; unplugging electrical appliances, raising everything in the garage and driving our cars to higher ground. I took flasks of coffee upstairs along with extra toilet rolls and a dirt tray for the cat. However, after an hour, the water suddenly subsided, leaving horrible sludge like a dark beige blanket over everything.

We were devastated for our neighbours. We only knew their first names (they had recently moved in) and had no way of contacting them. When they did arrive home with their two small children, I directed them into our drive and brought them inside while they tried to come to terms with everything, and after a while they drove off to stay with family.

We thought that it was a once in a lifetime occurrence. The insurance assessor had been next door, the fence panels were replaced, polluted belongings were taken away in a skip, and the piano went to restorers; the contractors were de-humidifying the house and the builders would be following – when on Friday 20 July the heavens delivered a monsoon!

This time the floodwater came higher, advancing once more up our drive. We repeated the precautionary steps. Then I did what any self-respecting WI member would have done and made a cake! It kept me calm while watching the fridge and freezers awaiting removal in No. 1's drive gaily bob around in floodwater.

About this time, our neighbour from No. 3 was collected from hospital, having had a new hip earlier in the week. The poor man couldn't get across the bridge, so was driven to relations in another part of Cheltenham, returning six hours later when the flood subsided.

Our neighbours are still in rented accommodation (and probably will be until the end of the year). The maintenance team have extracted 100 gallons of water out of the walls, but would you believe it, in their garden dear little flowers are still thriving!

Shirley Carter

Uckington & Elmstone Hardwicke WI

Between noon and 2 p.m. the water rose 4ft making the lane impassable and flooding our yard, paddock, garden and garage. The drains couldn't take the deluge and surplus water ran down the main A4019 like a river, flooding houses in its path. Our front wall was knocked down by waves from vehicles trying to get through, not succeeding and then backing out. A ladder from our Dutch barn was found on the main road the next day. We have never known floods this high before. It took about three days to clear, but my front garden took about a week.

Looking across from the house to the yard gate and lane with the garden in the foreground. (Shirley Carter)

Mary Walker

Toddington WI

Fortunately, the water only came up to our doorsills, but the manor opposite had its cellar flooded and the bridleway up the hill became a raging torrent. We hadn't seen anything like it in thirty-five years. The water reached the road and became a fast flowing river, with mud and debris collecting on the corner making an impassable dam. Our village is at the foot of Alderton Hill, so the houses backing onto the hill were all affected. The water flowed through garages and floodwater was 6ft deep in houses opposite the school.

The occupants of one house had gone on holiday to Australia for six weeks only the day before, but volunteers soon started bailing out and saving what they could. All roads into the village were flooded and the bridge over Carrant

The White Hart in Maisemore, with the road – now a river – running alongside. (Jill Beddoe)

The view from Maisemore – with meadows turned into lakes. (Jill Beddoe)

Brook lost its supporting wall. Children coming home from school were led over this flood in single file, all holding hands as the current was so strong. Our local farmer came to the rescue with his digger, and transported several stranded villagers over the floodwater in the bucket. About thirty stranded people stayed in the B&B on the main road overnight. One lady was taken ill but paramedics managed to reach her to take her to hospital. Four bowsers were quickly organised when the water supply ran out, bottled water was distributed throughout the village by volunteers in each road, and the village shop was kept busy supplying us with essentials.

Adine Keatley

Willersey WI

In Willersey, thirty-six houses were flooded with 2ft of water. All roads into the village became impassable causing people to abandon cars and stay in outlying village halls or scout huts. The Bell Inn put thirty-eight people up overnight.

Carole Bevan

Tibberton & Taynton WI

What a week! Tuesday 17 July was a normal day until about 11a.m. Then the rain got heavier, a tremendous wind suddenly blew up and within thirty seconds the village had experienced a mini tornado. Slates were ripped from the church roof, branches torn from trees. The destruction ended at the Mushroom Farm where a barn was severely damaged, a half-ton skip moved over a hundred yards and an old oak tree was ripped from the ground. ITV despatched their cameras and the village found itself on the evening news!

Friday brought heavy, continuous rain and some villagers didn't get home that evening. Others abandoned their vehicles at the end of the lane and waded through waist-high water, while some took the footpath through Bovone Farm.

On Saturday morning we found ourselves imprisoned in the village, with no access to the Gloucester–Newent road at Rudford. Only tractors and 4×4 vehicles could attempt the main lane to Taynton, which was completely awash with water. However, one young lady, dressed in a skirt, braved the water on her bicycle, as she had rabbits to feed! The village hall was opened for residents to store furniture or use in any other way as water flooded lower lying properties. Wildlife drowned, crops were devastated and fences were flattened. Youngsters, however, revelled in all the water!

Dorothy Womersley
Winchcombe WI

I was devastated when I saw water covering our back garden. We couldn't stop water coming into the conservatory but with a neighbour's help tried to stop it getting into the garage with buckets. Then another neighbour arrived with a pump. By now the water was 2ft deep outside, and rushing like a raging torrent down the drive and over the road. We managed to keep the lounge dry, but water got under the floorboards via the airbricks. We're still waiting to be dried out.

Maggie Vinson
Woodmancote WI

My 80-year-old mum lives in Kelmscott. The Water Board opened the sluice gates at Lechlade on Saturday 21 July, following eighteen hours of torrential rain, and part of the hamlet was flooded. My mother's house is in a private road, which became a raging river.

Nine weeks before, my mother slipped on the stairs and broke her hip. She was making an amazing recovery when the flood hit, and then had another

Sandbags at cottage doors in Vineyard Street, Winchcombe. (Alan Herod)

bad fall on it. She wouldn't let an air ambulance be called and spent the next four days in bed in great pain.

The house had just been sold as Mum is moving to France to live with my brother and his wife. She thought this was the end of her dream. My husband and I couldn't get to her for a week and only then because we have a four-wheel drive vehicle. We made several calls each day, and Mum kept telling us she was OK! Neighbours were very good. One had a new car delivered at the other end of the village, but couldn't get it home for over a week. A local farmer ferried people to the edge of the flood with his tractor so the new car could be used to get to Lechlade for supplies.

Ten days later, Mum was taken to hospital where her hip was x-rayed, and thankfully she only had severe bruising. Her buyers came to see her the next day and said they still wanted the house. They know the village and accepted that this was a freak occurrence.

Maggie Drake
Yew Trees WI

Because of its altitude, Painswick was hardly affected by the flooding, except for several wool mills, now converted into dwellings, sited along the Painswick stream.

On Friday afternoon, the stream became a raging torrent, in some places 30 to 40yd wide, carrying tree branches, rocks and other debris, and leaving havoc and destruction in its wake. Where it passed Painswick Mill, the surging, muddy floodwater raced over the road bridge as well as underneath it. Cotswold stone walls, some possibly standing for hundreds of years, were washed away in a matter of minutes, while concrete driveways were gouged out and railings flattened or mangled. A large fridge freezer was bobbing around in the millpond like a cork, after being hurled downstream. The cellars and basements of the mills were awash, having not recovered from flooding only weeks before.

Marian Enstone
Bredon WI

We did suffer some storm damage on Friday 20 July. Returning home from the supermarket, we found a sooty, slimy stream trickling down the walls of the inglenook fireplace, ending in a black puddle on the lounge carpet. In our semi-basement utility room (2ft 6in below ground level) our white goods were standing in eight inches of water and the Dyson was bobbing around like a cork. We also had wet floors, soggy carpets and damp walls in our guest cottage.

A month on, the fans and de-humidifier are still running around the clock drying the place out.

chapter four

RESCUED

Joan Jordan

Minsterworth WI

I am a patient at the Cotswold Dialysis Unit at Gloucestershire Royal Hospital (GRH), attending three days a week for four-hour sessions. On the Monday after the floods I was told there would be no dialysis at the hospital as they had no electricity or water and emergency arrangements were being made. Later I was told I would be picked up between 7 p.m. and 9 p.m., possibly by fire engine, as the A48 into Gloucester was impassable.

Imagine my surprise when the RAF Rescue Service rang asking my exact whereabouts – they were coming to pick me up by helicopter! They asked us to go onto the road and wave something bright so they could see us. My husband, an ex-Navy man, promptly fetched his Red Duster Flag but the police arrived on the scene and stood each side of the A48 with their bright yellow jackets, ready to signal to the helicopter. Two police cars stopped the traffic and everyone was watching skyward to spot the helicopter. It was twenty minutes before it flew overhead and turned, then flew down the road and landed 25yd from our house. It was a Sea King, much larger than I expected.

BBC Top Gear *presenter Richard Hammond donned his wetsuit and rescued his friends Zog and Gill Ziegler from their home near Haw Bridge. Their house had been flooded with 6ft of water.* (Anne Turner)

A policewoman put her arm around me and said, 'Right Joan, here we go, keep your head down or the draught will make your hair stand on end!' One of the crew fitted me with earphones, escorted me to the door and helped me in. I was surprised at how big it was inside, with seats along the sides, just like you see in the war films with troops going into action! There were two more patients I knew from Upleadon and Newent and I soon forgot my nerves as we took off.

At the Waterwells Industrial Estate at Quedgeley, by the new police headquarters, they opened the side door and lowered one of the crew out until only his feet were left inside the helicopter. This looked really hairy, but he was hooked up from his back to the inside roof. He placed a marker on the ground, they winched him back in, and we landed. Transport was waiting to take us to GRH where all the Monday dialysis patients were assembling.

There are approximately 200 patients a week needing treatment, and staff had worked all day arranging where patients could receive it, as well as organising transport to get them into Gloucester and to hospitals in the Midlands and then back home again: a mammoth task to be repeated every day until the emergency was over.

We eventually left Gloucester at 10.15 p.m. Ten of us went to Stratford-on-Avon to have our treatment at midnight after the local patients had finished and the machines had been prepared. Some also went to Tipton, Walsall, Kings Norton and Birmingham. Our Gloucester nursing staff went with us. After treatment, patients were transported back to GRH, arriving between 6 a.m. and 7 a.m.

John Coopey from Woodmancote (left) with the dialysis patients he drove from Gloucester to Stratford for treatment. (Yvonne Coopey)

Unfortunately, I was taken ill at Stratford and ended up in Warwick Hospital until the following Thursday evening, and then had to travel through more flooding on the way home. I was taken from Warwick to Stratford on the Wednesday for my treatment at midnight.

On Friday I went to Walsall, and again on the following Monday, then back to Stratford on the Wednesday and Friday. By this time everyone was getting very tired, and we were so pleased to hear that the Cotswold Unit would be open again the following Monday. Tankers would bring in water until the Unit water was passed fit. The NHS certainly pulled out all the stops to make sure we got our lifesaving treatment.

Kathleen Willoughby

Sedgeberrow WI

At 3.30 p.m. we had a flood warning from the Environment Agency, so we carried as much as possible upstairs. From there I could see the water rushing across the orchard, and within minutes it came into the house with such force that we had to retreat upstairs ourselves. We could hear the furniture and china crashing about. My son called for help and we were asked to drop down from the bedroom window into the rescue boat, but as I am 86 years old, and my husband 87, we felt that that was impossible. A helicopter was then called and we were airlifted to safety. Friends then kindly looked after us. We had 5ft of water in our house and lost almost everything. It was a very frightening experience.

Vera Topham

Norton WI

Staverton Airport is at the front of our house and the helicopters – Sea Kings etc. – were constantly flying overhead to refuel. What a good job they did!

Velma Sutton

Apperley & Deerhurst WI

One day we went back down the hill to our flooded cottage to discover an emergency forces boat in the water outside our gate and a helicopter hovering overhead. There'd been concern about neighbours along the riverbank whose house was surrounded by water, but a friend had already turned up in a boat the evening before and rescued them.

The Severn Area Rescue Association team off to rescue flood victims in Tirley. (Anne Turner)

Firemen taking a quick rest between rescues at Gabb Lane, Apperley. (Rose Williams)

Anne Turner
Ashleworth & Hasfield WI

We heard a very loud noise overhead. Outside, a yellow Sea King helicopter lowered a winchman to a bungalow. The stretcher came down and someone was removed to hospital. It was quite an experience to watch. The helicopter's powerful searchlights lit up the centre of the village and it looked almost like a spaceship. The crew pinpointed the bungalow and showed their skills in working under awful conditions in pitch darkness. The injured man had a nasty head wound and a broken wrist but he's home again now, much recovered.

Dorothy Day
Moreton-in-Marsh WI

I'm 85 and live in a retirement complex in Moreton-in-Marsh. It had been raining hard all week. No way could I go out, so after lunch I settled down to watch television. At 2.15 p.m. there was a loud banging on my French windows and the manager shouted to me to get upstairs quickly. I glanced into the kitchen and saw a big pool of water. Not thinking, I opened the front door to speak to him and water rushed past. I managed to shut the door and then from upstairs I could see about nine inches of water rushing in. When it was covering all the hydrangea bushes outside I started to worry and telephoned my daughter in Upper Slaughter, but she was blocked by flooding.

At 4.30 p.m. I looked down my stairs and saw china floating about. The water was about 2ft deep. By 6.30 p.m. there was no one about, it was still raining and the water level had risen above the sundial and was covering most of the bushes in the garden. I put the light on in the bedroom to show I was there.

By 8.15 p.m. the water was up to my fifth stair. When I saw four firemen helping a neighbour into a boat, I shouted for help. 'OK we'll be with you in ten

Pedestrians being helped across the road by firemen at the Swan Inn, Moreton-in-Marsh.
(Chic Dempster)

minutes. Get a bag packed.' Relief at last! Two firemen carried me downstairs, put me into a boat, and pushed two of us out – hitting bushes and hidden garden ornaments on the way. Eight of us were helped into a van and evacuated to the Fire Service College, given food and a room for the night. Everyone was so kind. The firemen really deserve a medal. They were soaking wet and looked very tired.

After breakfast the next morning, most people were rescued by friends or relatives, though some remained another night at the college. Now all the residents at the retirement complex have been evacuated to friends, relatives or hotels. It will be some time before our homes are habitable again.

Ursula Groves-Smith
Staunton & District WI

Some of my family were rescued during the night by the rescue service at Deerhurst when their home was flooded with 4ft of water. Their house will not be liveable for months, with plaster off the walls and floorboards ripped up. They have to live in a mobile home. I have raided my cupboards for plates, dishes, cups and saucers. They have lost everything downstairs; fridges, freezers, washing machines etc. It is a nightmare for them and their neighbours.

Anonymous
Tibberton & Taynton WI

Mum (94) recently moved from Scotland to Tewkesbury. Seven weeks later her adventure began! The waters began to rise around the Sheltered Housing, and by next morning the ground floor flats were flooded. The Fire Service took everyone to the local council offices and they were given a numbered evacuee badge. Mum and three ladies, along with provisions, airbeds and blankets, were taken by bus to the Heywood Centre in Cinderford where they spent the night. I eventually found out she was en route to the Dilke Hospital. The ladies only had the clothes they stood up in, so with the help of a charity shop in Newent and a kindly neighbour, I managed to find a new wardrobe for them all. Mum and her friends, aged between 70 and 95, never lost their sense of humour. She's now staying with us in Tibberton until her flat is refurbished. Her friends are temporarily housed in Newent.

Madeleine Jones
Winchcombe WI

We stopped at a garage on the way back from lunch in Bishops Cleeve. I got out of the car, somehow dislocating my knee. It was so painful we went to a B&B across the road. An ambulance was called, but took ages to arrive. They kept calling to say they were on their way but were having difficulty getting through.

I was finally taken to Cheltenham A&E, where it was hours before I was taken to a ward. I wasn't allowed food as they planned to operate on Saturday – then Sunday. Still no food. On Sunday night I was given a little food and a drink, as they now planned to operate on Monday. I was finally taken to theatre on Monday afternoon. When I came to I was very relieved that they had manipulated my knee, avoiding another knee replacement.

On Tuesday I was picked up by my son and taken home. It had been a very long time since I set out to go to lunch.

Trevor Humphries and Steve Eaton in a rescue boat in Sandhurst. (Rosemary Lyons)

chapter five

CHANGE OF PLAN

Sandra Hughes

Quedgeley WI

Little did we know as we prepared for our daughter Emma's wedding day in Quedgeley what impact the rain would have on the day we'd been planning for sixteen months.

Friday started with heavy rain but Emma arrived from her home in Swindon mid-morning with no problems, her car boot full of flowers for the church and lots of wedding bits and pieces. Her partner, Keiron, was following in a few hours with his mum Kate and sister Toria.

Emma, sister Siân and I, spent the afternoon at the church arranging flowers. Then came the phone calls – Keiron had left Swindon, but after two hours was still trying to get onto the A419 and Siân's fiancé, John, couldn't get further than Bristol by train because of flooding. The Bristol road from Gloucester was flooded and people everywhere were trying to get home. Siân and I decided to go to Bristol to collect John. We set off at 5.30 p.m. down the A38 – the M5 was blocked solid southbound, and we knew Keiron was stuck on it somewhere; he'd now been on the road for five hours!

Emma and Keiron Skillett on their wedding day. (Sandra Hughes)

I've never driven through floodwater as deep as on the A38 through Whitminster. I had a fairly high car, but it still came to the top of my wheels at times, sometimes 3ft deep – very frightening. Siân was giving me advice and sounded as if she'd done this many times but then informed me she'd once read it in the Highway Code!

An hour later we managed to get back onto the M5 at junction 13 and the rest of our journey was uneventful, but we knew Keiron was in a much smaller car now travelling the other way up the A38. He made it eventually, after six hours. We got back from Bristol after a three-hour round trip, not too bad.

But things got worse. Emma had received calls from guests having major problems. Some were stuck on the M5, some in the Evesham rescue centre and some from Leicester had turned back to try again tomorrow. We went to bed to the sound of helicopters flying to and fro overhead, rescuing stranded people and taking them to the police headquarters at Waterwells.

Next morning, there was light rain and we had fingers crossed it would stop by the time Emma left for the church at 11.45 a.m. Guests started arriving. The record journey was Kirsten and Lee taking twenty-one hours to drive from Newcastle: five to get to Birmingham, then sixteen to get to Quedgeley! Some people arrived just minutes before the wedding and in the end only six didn't make it. Noon arrived, the rain stopped, and later, when we got to Eastwood Park for the reception, the sun came out in time for the photographs.

Stella Lainchbury
Berkeley WI

Two friends and I had booked a coach trip to the Cotswolds. We managed coffee in a restaurant at Lechlade, then the road starting flooding and the coach driver decided to get onto higher ground to get us back to Dursley. Floods all the way – no trouble for the coach! I picked up my car, but the A38 – my lifeline to home – was closed due to floods. A detour up on to higher ground was the answer. I joined a queue of traffic trying to force its way through a short distance of flooding 4–5ft deep. My only choice was to take a chance or spend the night in the car. I took the chance – never again! I'm 88 years old!

Marian Enstone

Bredon WI

We were on a 'mercy mission' delivering milk to friends who'd had water creeping across the garden and lapping around their doors. Our route took us from Bredon via the M5 to Cheltenham, along the Tewkesbury road and up the A38 to Tewkesbury. Near the Tewkesbury Park Hotel we saw young boys in wellies paddling and pedalling their bicycles through the murky waters. Trundling down the hill from the hotel was a large yellow truck with about a dozen passengers – hotel guests with their baggage and golf clubs departing in style! They'd arrived at the hotel on Friday expecting to spend a few pleasant days on the golf course, but instead had spent the entire weekend trapped inside the hotel. The yellow vehicle turned out to be a waste skip transporter – minus the skip of course!

No holidaying in these caravans at The Fleet, Twyning. (Margaret Bailey)

A change of mooring site for this boat on the Avon near Tewkesbury. (Tony Price)

Jean Tebbett

Central Cheltenham WI

It's still raining. After a disturbed night of thunder and lightning I wonder if it will ever stop? I'm attending WI Craft at St Luke's Church Hall this afternoon; so I put on my wellies and mac, grab my umbrella and set off on a ten-minute walk. On the way I notice Sandford Park looks a bit puddly, I hope it doesn't flood like it did a month ago. I arrive at the hall with dry feet but rather soggy jeans.

We settle down to make Christmas things for our October sales table. We notice cars coming down the rather narrow street outside the hall and turning into Sandford Street (also narrow and one way) going up it the wrong way. Some are doing three point turns and not knowing where to go. We think we should go home so we clear away the tables. Back on with the rain gear. Outside the hall, a driver asks if he can leave his car there. He can't get into College Road where he lives.

I look down the road and realise I won't be able to get across Bath Parade which has become a fast flowing river. Gingerly, I walk along Sandford Street, which comes out onto Bath Road opposite the Playhouse. The water is lapping up to the edge of the street. I cross over and walk along Oriel Road and eventually cross over again to Rodney Road, the water deep in the gutters. I walk through Cambray. It seems odd to see traffic crawling through the pedestrian precinct by Beechwood. My ten-minute walk home takes forty minutes.

We're just about to sit down to our evening meal at 6 p.m. when our son walks in. He left Sudeley at 1.30 p.m. Unable to get home to Sedgeberrow he came to us. His wife calls to say helicopters are overhead rescuing people from their homes. It's waist deep outside the school and Winchcombe Road is impassable. Our granddaughter's also been trying to get home from work. The police walk with her car through the flooded road they're about to close to save her spending the night in Pittville Pump Room. We go for a walk in the evening. The rain has almost stopped. Helicopters are cruising low overhead, using the college cricket ground to land.

Joy Bradley

Gotherington, Woolstone & Oxenton WI

I'd arranged to visit my Vice President, Lyn, and Secretary, Pat, in Gotherington to go through the agenda for our meeting the following Wednesday, which Lyn was chairing because I was expecting two Japanese students to arrive that evening. When I left Pat's at noon the water was four inches deep in the lane, but I got home safely.

The water went off and I decided to cancel our Wednesday meeting. 'Host families' started to ring the coordinator to say they couldn't take the students. That left a mammoth task for the coordinator to find alternative homes.

I ended up with three fifteen-year-old girls who didn't speak much English. I told them that when they went to the toilet, if they only did a wee, not to flush the toilet. When needed, they could flush and then tell us so we could refill the cistern using water from butts in the garden. They watched to see what was involved and were very good.

The water butts were emptying but more rain was forecast. My husband emptied the water into anything he could lay his hands on. The rains came again on Friday, completely refilling the butts. We then managed to get by without using the bowsers until water was restored. Drinking water was a different thing! At first it was very difficult to obtain, but once a system was in place everything was fine.

I think the girls relished getting away with a 'cat's lick'. The water came on briefly and the girls had showers, but when it was our turn the water was gone again and we were back to a couple of bowls in the bath!

Sue Mills
Ashmead Green WI

During the day of heavy rain we were either cruising the River Avon on our narrow boat *Shiraz* or moored to a floating pontoon in Tewkesbury Marina. We left Strensham lock, north of Tewkesbury, at 11 a.m. and made the two-hour journey to our home mooring in torrential rain with rising river levels. Our original plan was to enjoy Tewkesbury's Water Festival, which was cancelled, so we decided to sit it out rather than cut short our break. While all the boats in the marina remained safe, our parked car was unfortunately overcome by 3ft of water!

Jill Parsons
Gotherington, Woolstone & Oxenton WI

My Canadian cousin, Gail, and her husband, neither of whom I'd met before, were paying their first visit to Britain. They spent a few days with my sister and her partner in Wiltshire, who were bringing them to meet me. My brother, Chris, came down from York ready to take them back with him. I had a lovely lunch planned. As a bonus, my daughter Jane was bringing her seven-day-old twins over.

The Wiltshire contingent arrived in heavy rain and I started to make coffee. It was at that point that my sister announced that a wave of water was flowing down my garden. I live in a beautiful position in Woodmancote with a small garden backing on to open hillside. A little stream, often dry in summer, runs along my rear boundary. The volume of water flowing down from the hill was too much for the stream to accommodate and it was heading towards my bungalow, at the lowest point in a small cul-de-sac.

This had happened on a smaller scale three weeks earlier so I knew what to do. Donning wellies and mac, I opened the side gates and the back and front

Chris and Mark digging trenches across Jill's garden to stop the water flooding into the house. (Jill Parsons)

garage doors to let the water through. This time, however, it wasn't enough. Chris and Mark joined me in torrential rain, digging trenches across my garden, using turf as 'sandbags' to protect the patio doors and then building a barricade with garden benches, patio pots, seed trays – anything they could find.

The water continued to flow and at some point, my lovely lunch forgotten, my sister foraged and made sandwiches. Had I been alone, I couldn't have prevented the flood. As it was, it went through the airbricks and up under the wooden floors giving me damp carpets, which I could live with until they dried out.

Chris left with my cousin and her husband mid-afternoon. When they realised how widespread the problems were they tried to turn back but couldn't get back into the village. They spent thirteen hours in the car, mostly in Gloucestershire, before getting home. Mark spent the afternoon wrapped in a duvet while his clothes steamed on the radiator. When he and Jane tried to leave, the lane was a raging torrent, so they stayed.

I'd barely had time to talk to my cousin, but my abiding memory will be standing in the bathroom, with Gail and Jane, gazing into the loo which had filled up with water backed up from the main drainage system. We estimated that perhaps there was room for just one person to wee in it. In the spirit of true WI hospitality we gave the privilege to Gail!

Betty Welch

Norton WI

My husband, Bryan, was helping Tewkesbury Art Society set up their annual exhibition at the Methodist Hall at the Cross. Our MP, Lawrence Robertson, had agreed to open the event and food and wine were organised.

*Not many tourists!
Tewkesbury had become
an island cut off by the
floods.* (Philippa Keen)

Due to the
floods we will
be closed until
further notice.
Sorry for any
inconvenience
caused.

*Hundreds of businesses and shops were forced to close
due to flood damage. Many may never reopen.*
(Matilda Pearce)

*Tibberton Mushroom
Farm had been hit by a
tornado earlier in the
week and now had to
face another disaster.*
(Phil Bevan)

Business is definitely not blooming at Barbers Bridge Nurseries at Rudford. (Phil Bevan)

Ronsons Reclamation Centre in Sandhurst immersed in floodwater. (Jennie Moss)

Bryan left the hall around 1.30 p.m. The road outside Morrisons was awash with floodwater and it took some time to turn on to the bypass. (Some of his colleagues who left later took over three hours to travel the same route; others didn't get home at all.) The A38 was flooded at Coombe Hill and nearer Norton he had to mount the pavement to pass through floods.

We apprehensively watched our road become flooded, though our home was well out of harm's way. About 5 p.m., Jane telephoned. She had the wine and most of the food and had tried every route but it was impossible to get out of Bredon. Bryan advised her to eat as much of the food as she could but not to overdo the wine! Mary and Penny lived in town and went to the hall just in case anyone turned up. Only one person did!

All the next week the exhibition remained closed. Penny was flooded in but Mary went in every day to check the pictures. The flooding had peaked ten inches below the hall floor.

They held the exhibition the following week, mornings only. The town was quiet with many shops and businesses closed and attendance was understandably low.

Margaret Stewart

Randwick WI

During the school holidays Randwick WI holds a sports day for village children. This was cancelled because we had no running water. Charity performances of Jane Austen's *Sense and Sensibility* over the weekend of 20/21 July in a local garden were re-scheduled. One of the actors spent the night in his car on the M5 while returning from his graduation ceremony at Liverpool University.

Valerie Martin

Gotherington, Woolstone & Oxenton WI

A Silver Wedding celebration was planned for Saturday 28 July in a marquee in the garden of Church Cottage. Guests who came from out of the county were asked to bring water, water and more water for washing-up between lunch and the evening party. It was an extremely happy occasion and, for villagers invited, gave them something positive to focus on.

The tragic scene in the flooded village of Oxenton.
(Valerie Martin)

chapter six

ANIMALS

Ivy Clayson

Ashleworth & Hasfield WI

Ashleworth is used to flooding, but not in July. I had taken my grandchildren riding and we went down to the water to paddle. We came across Jeremy and his son Rupert transferring a generator from the back of their car into a canoe to paddle it back to the manor house to help get the floodwater out. Some local farmers rallied around to help rescue some pigs. The hedges on the lower road have been left brown and dead looking but my lasting memory will be the thousands of dead worms left on the road as the floods receded.

Hazel Wheeler

Fairford WI

When I was flooded my cat went missing for two days. When he was found we took him with us to my son's house in the next road. While there he had to come to terms with the resident dog and cat. The dog was soon under control,

Tom Finch and Andy Shayle rescue some piglets in Ashleworth. (Paul Finch)

Mum swims to safety too! (Paul Finch)

Millie enjoys a swim! (Kate Ratcliffe)

but the two cats had several words. Five days later he made it very plain he wanted to go home, so he took himself off to more familiar territory and refused to budge. He now has a comfy bed in the greenhouse and access to the house, his adoring slaves coming to see him several times a day. As we found a present of a mouse in the kitchen this morning, I think he's settling down.

Jackie Turner

Forthampton WI

Did anyone else have a tortoise that survived the flooding, and if so do you know how they managed it?

By 4 p.m. on Friday 20 July our house was surrounded by water, and the back garden, supposedly 'tortoise proof', was knee-deep in water. My husband searched for ages for our tortoise, Charles, but to no avail and we feared the worst. The next morning we found him up by the fence, alive. A small miracle! We dried him off in the house during the following two days and he's now back in his piece of garden, none the worse for wear.

I wonder if tortoises, like cats, have nine lives? If so, Charles has certainly used up several of his!

Jacqui Taylor

Sandhurst WI

Flooding started in Sandhurst, where we used to live, on Sunday morning. By lunchtime the flood still hadn't peaked. Action was required, so family and friends with water-borne resources were called upon. Large canoes were mobilised and a posse of chaps set off to the landward end of the road into the village. The water was nearer to Gloucester than we had experienced in thirty years.

Two young men in the rescue team canoed up the lane. Where they passed under the raised bypass, the water was rushing through the bottleneck. They phoned the support group to say not to follow. They

Chickens from Wallsworth Lodge in Sandhurst were ferried across the flooding in large boxes. (Ray Bullock)

The chickens were then loaded onto a trolley and taken to a stable at Wallsworth Farm where they quickly settled and laid a rewarding number of eggs! (Ray Bullock)

noticed the water was flowing from the floodplain towards the river: it was surface water drainage and not the river fuelling the flood.

At one point urgent action was needed. Ducks, hens and turkeys, who normally lived in rural bliss, were in trouble. In particular, two ducks sitting on eggs needed to be moved to a dry location. Without ado, the ducks and their nests were decanted by hand into the canoe and borne across the flood to the nearest dry land. The Ark arrived safely, new nest sites were identified and the young families relocated.

Rescuing ducks from a flood – that makes this flood unique for us!

Rosemary Lyons
Sandhurst WI

Five of us had been to Northamptonshire to see our grandson, home from his gap year travels. On our return we found all three routes into Sandhurst blocked by deep floodwater, so we decided to stay the night at my daughter's. Next day we set off again, passing lots of abandoned cars as we got nearer home. Our farmyard and some barns had been flooded but luckily the cattle yards were safe.

A few days later, when the Severn flooded and our water was cut off, our main concern was getting water to the 250 cattle in the barns. We had to use a slurry tanker to suck water out of a pond and fill all the tanks – a time consuming business. They drank 1,400 gallons a day – and a few small fish!

Our son-in-law was helping a friend rescue people and animals from the deep water at the lower end of the village in a canoe when they went over a completely submerged car. They forced cattle to swim to higher ground and then took two people and their dog from their cottage to a nearby farm to safety.

Tibberton Animal Rescue.
(Phil Bevan)

Christine Crane

Tibberton & Taynton WI

The Fire Brigade arrived in the early hours of Saturday at our boarding kennels and cattery. They made up concrete platforms to keep the dogs above the rising water. The cattle in the adjoining field were also moved across the road to safety. Twenty-four dogs were taken to safety in temporary homes around the village. Five or six cats found themselves moved up into the bedrooms in my house. Cheltenham Animal Shelter later came to rescue all the animals, who are now safely back with their owners none the worse for their experience, and the business is up and running again. I am now living in a mobile home in the garden, my home not likely to be habitable for some months.

Maureen Haines

Tibberton & Taynton WI

We housed several dogs from the kennels, which my husband Tony rescued with his tractor and stock cage. The first dog was a tiny white one, very cold and frightened. Within one hour we rescued five dogs of varying sizes and dried and fed them.

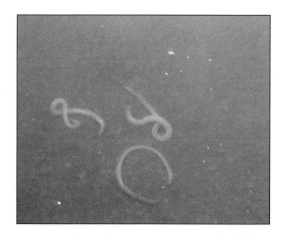

Masses of worms accumulated on the public bridleway in Apperley. (Rose Williams)

Julia Walker
Toddington WI

Our farmhouse was flooded all through the ground floor. We had sandbags at the doors but it came up through the parquet floors, which were floating, and left a lovely jigsaw puzzle when the water subsided. I had an elderly basset hound which tried to keep out of the water by climbing on to the logs at the side of the wood-burning stove, but sadly later drowned after having an epileptic fit underwater.

Yvette Mates
Norton WI

At Abloads Court, in the lower part of Sandhurst, the owners took their horses into the house as they were totally surrounded by water. Many farmers had to throw away milk once their bulk tanks were full as the milk tankers couldn't reach them. Some had to send their animals for slaughter because there was nowhere to keep them, and others literally 'farmed out' their livestock to people who had land and buildings above the flood-line. Some animals drowned. Enormous areas of crops of grass and corn have been ruined, leaving many with no grazing and no winter feed.

chapter seven

BOTTLES, BOWSERS AND SPRINGS

Southfield WI Members

Bowser! How many of us knew what it meant, let alone had heard the word before the floods? Suddenly everyone was talking about them and overnight it became the latest 'in' word for 2007. Is it full or empty? Who decided where to put them? Where had they come from originally? Who spotted the red and yellow ones?

Instead of greeting people with 'weather talk' it was 'water talk': Have you been flooded? Are you okay for water? Where's the nearest bowser?

Cooking became more imaginative: trying to use less water and the minimum number of pots and utensils to save on washing-up. Hooray for microwaves!

The parable of turning water into wine came true: water kindly donated from a water butt to a neighbour came back as a bottle of wine.

It made us appreciate how much water it takes to flush a loo and how heavy it is to carry.

We discovered that tea made with bottled water tastes better than tap water, and that washing in rainwater makes hair and skin feel softer.

The Mythe water treatment plant in Tewkesbury (in the foreground) became flooded and had to be shut down on Sunday 22 July. The reservoirs then ran dry and 150,000 homes in Gloucestershire were without running water for nearly two weeks. (Jennie Moss)

Jean Tebbett

Central Cheltenham WI

On Sunday 22 July I heard there was going to be a water shortage so I filled up the bath and phoned our next-door neighbour, who was in London. I asked him to bring some bottled water back (the shops had been cleared of water, milk etc.) and whether he wanted his bath filling? What a nightmare finding

Collecting water from a bowser became a regular chore. This one was at Swindon Village in Cheltenham.
(Sara Jefferies)

Water bowsers became a common site on the streets of Gloucestershire during the water shortage. (Matilda Pearce)

the bowsers empty; going to wash your hands only to find no water in the taps; the loo looking disgusting and wondering if it will ever be clean again. What joy when the water came back on, even though it would be a while before it was safe to drink.

Margaret Stewart

Randwick WI

On the Monday we heard on BBC Radio Gloucestershire that our water supply was running dry. Our neighbour immediately topped up his hot tub and invited people nearby to use this for flushing toilets etc. It was a great resource, as a bowser didn't arrive in the village until the following Sunday.

WI initiative at work!

Esme Anderson

The Village, Charlton Kings WI

During the water shortage we managed well. My husband Richard had worked in the Australian outback and was used to water rationing. He seemed to relish soaping up in the garden and getting me to rinse him off with a watering can filled from the water butt – very bracing!

Penny White

Winstone WI

We were truly fortunate living in Whiteway, near Miserden, at the top of the Cotswold Hills with our own supply of water for flushing loos from the Holybrook stream. We only lost water for one day as our supply comes from the Birdlip Reservoir, fed by Thames Water in the crisis.

Anne Turner

Ashleworth & Hasfield WI

There was a knock on my front door with a request to open Tirley Village Hall for a delivery of bottled water by Tewkesbury Council. Notices were put up around the village to say water could be collected between 8 a.m. and 10 a.m. and 5 p.m. and 6 p.m. each day. Whenever water was delivered people came out of the woodwork to unload the lorries – including two deliveries by the army at 10 p.m. Neighbours took it upon themselves to look after the elderly or those with young children, and our Village Agent worked tirelessly to help

The chain-gang unloading bottled water at Tirley Village Hall. (Anne Turner)

Bottles were stored in Tirley Village Hall to await collection by residents. (Anne Turner)

vulnerable people. I met villagers I hadn't spoken to for years and also new people in the village.

One man, not having any milk, put wine on his cornflakes, and another turned up every day with his wheelbarrow to take his bottled water home. An elderly man, who came part of the way by boat, sat chatting before returning home. One day when the army delivered water we provided them with coffee and biscuits. Another time they had a high vehicle and went through the floodwater to take water to residents living upstairs in flooded homes at Haw Bridge. We also sent them milk, bread and papers. Everyone rallied round and it was good to see some of that 'wartime spirit'.

The Army were brought in to help speed up delivery of water supplies. (Anne Turner)

Clare Smith

Birdlip & Brimpsfield WI

I live at the almshouses in Painswick and had quite overlooked the fact that I was classed as 'elderly'. Listening to local radio, the message went out for folk to make sure that vulnerable neighbours had water to drink. Our local reservoir is only three minutes walk away – I was going to be alright.

Then came a volunteer delivering water in canisters. I had four. My son-in-law arrived with a churn of water, a large container to bail it into, and a small calf-feeding bucket to use for flushing the toilet. Then came a ring at the doorbell. There stood a drowned looking young man wearing a big smile and a halo – as worn by those doing good deeds. 'I've brought you some bottles of water'. 'Thank you,' I said, 'Put them down here'.

There followed two days of unsolicited deliveries of bottled water, by which time I almost dreaded my doorbell ringing. I had sixty-two bottles of water, a churn and six water containers, and nowhere to store them.

Meanwhile, someone discovered a water bowser parked by the local 'God's Acre' – the cemetery, and if there were any residents who didn't need water, it was those dear souls!

I couldn't lift the packs of bottles so I attacked the polythene around one pack with my vegetable knife to haul out a bottle. The top was on tight, so I jammed it between the open door and the woodwork, squeezed the door shut and turned the bottle. Next second I had water everywhere, over the floor and myself. But I had won! I wandered about around packs of bottles in my small kitchen. They went in single file around the furniture.

That day, I needed to put in a repeat prescription at the local surgery. The smiling receptionist came up to the counter, felt underneath and brought out a pack of small bottles of water. 'Here you are Mrs Smith – some individual bottles. Easier to deal with.' Not for ME! I couldn't carry a pack of twelve bottles home up the hill. I backed away, carefully, shaking my head. 'I have plenty thank you.'

That evening came a ring at my door. I negotiated the packs of bottles across my kitchen floor toward the front door; a smiling gentleman with a bright good deed halo presented me with a pack of twenty-four small bottles of water!

It's three weeks since the floods. I now have water in my tap – it has a flavour of swimming pool water, but I can use my supply of 'bottled' for tea and coffee. I'm glad to say I'm now down to sixteen large bottles, eighteen small and half a churn of water plus half a butt of rainwater!

Diana Le Clair

Central Cheltenham WI

At the moment it's tipping down with rain so I'm guaranteed loo-flushing water from my water butt for a few days if I'm reasonably frugal. There's a bowser by the shop and so far we've got plenty in bottles for drinking. Laundry is on hold and it's amazing how good a 'shower' one can have with a washing-up bowl of hot water and a plastic jug! I walked up to the racecourse to look at the impressive rows of tankers filling up to replenish the bowsers. I admire the work and organisation all this has entailed – yet people still moan.

Six million litres of water a day were brought into the county. The Army are seen here unloading bottled water at Cheltenham Racecourse. It was then taken by lorry to various distribution points. (Sara Jefferies)

A huge Army water tank at Cheltenham Racecourse, which was used to fill smaller tankers refilling bowsers. (Sara Jefferies)

Ann Mills
Leonard Stanley WI

My 19-year-old grandson and his family in Quedgeley were without water for nearly two weeks. They managed by scooping water out of the canal with a bucket into a large container, supplemented by water from the rainwater butt. They used this for flushing the loo.

My elderly aunt and uncle in Churchdown were without water for two weeks. They had strip washes every day using water from the rainwater butt, which they also used to flush the loo, and for hand washing of 'smalls' in the sink.

Ann Parkin
The Village, Charlton Kings WI

A shower can easily be made by using an old washing-up bowl, three inches of warm water and a good helping of bath foam. You also need someone to stand higher than the bather and shower them with a soaked flannel.

Pat Hearne
Leonard Stanley WI

My grandson and his girlfriend live in Churchdown. They were without power for a day, managing with candles and a camping stove, and without water for two weeks. Simon works in an outlet depot and travels to work on a motorbike.

Carol Robinson returning home through floods in Sandhurst after collecting her bottled water.
(Margaret Collins)

This was an advantage as he could still manoeuvre between abandoned cars and, after trying several routes, get home. At work they avoided flooding, but watched the water rise three inches in half an hour. He was impressed by the police, handing out water to motorists from bus pull-ins. He advised some youngsters of the dangers of playing in the water and they remarked, 'I wondered what the smell was!'

Yvette Mates

Norton WI

I live at the top of the hill in Sandhurst. It felt a bit like living on Mount Ararat! The lower part of Sandhurst flooded to a depth of 7ft, with 110 houses damaged. Both roads out were impassable to cars for six days. We had no running water for eight days, and no electricity for over a day.

On Sunday 22 July I learned from the lunchtime news that the Mythe water pumping station had been deluged by floodwater and shut down. I filled as many containers as I could with water and by midnight my taps had run dry.

On Monday the 23rd the power went off. A neighbour invited me and a few others to join them and visitors from Bermuda to drink champagne by candlelight. We had a lovely evening, but after several glasses my bladder was full and I had to commit the worst possible social *faux pas*: to ask if I could use their loo! I felt terribly guilty because I knew they had to walk several hundred yards to a pond to fill buckets to flush their loos. They were extremely gracious, and like all good guests, I didn't flush for a wee! The electricity came back on in the early hours of Tuesday, but my fridge had defrosted itself all over my kitchen floor!

On Friday I was invited by friends in Hasfield, who have their own bore-hole water supply, for supper and a bath. Normally this would be a short journey but I had to go via the M5 and M50, which made it an eighty-mile round trip! A high bank had collapsed in their village resulting in a landslip, which blocked the road. Fortunately, a farmer with his tractor cleared this minutes before I arrived. Their bathroom had a spectacular 'sea view'.

On Sunday the 29th I went to friends in Minsterworth for lunch and a bath. It was a beautiful sunny day, but driving over the northern Gloucester bypass with the windows open, the stench from the sodden brown fields was over-powering.

My neighbours were away in Florida but their builder had left two large wheelbarrows and a large plastic container in their drive, which filled to the brim with rainwater and provided enough water to flush my loos for a week!

On Tuesday the 31st, the Army brought us supplies of bottled water in a tall lorry and on Wednesday 1 August, my neighbour borrowed a Landrover and drove 'over the top' to do a communal shop.

Monica Cook

Randwick WI

Along with several hillside villages bordering Stroud, we lost our water supply. We were promised a bowser, which didn't arrive for several days, but we had bottled water. Our water comes from a reservoir in Birdlip, which was used to help other parts of the county – until it ran out and we were all minus the precious liquid!

Luckily we have some natural water springs and people made use of these. There could have been a bad accident when a car, parked without its brakes fully on, ran down a slope and flipped over landing right in the 'Mayor's Pool', one of the places where people had been collecting spring water!

There was some damage locally in Puckshole. A sodden bank collapsed together with a few trees across the road, which remains closed.

Major distribution points were set up for bottled water like this one at Tesco in Gloucester, manned by volunteers and police. (Jill Beddoe)

Diana Colbeck
Southfield WI

When local bowsers dried up, the council eventually promised bottled water. Frantic phone calls were made for local helpers to offload the lorry. Eager volunteers turned up, along with an army of police officers. Eventually the lorry arrived and the chain-gang got to work, storing the precious bottles in the Social Centre. Those waiting for water joined in the gang and a real community spirit emerged.

Next morning distribution began, slowly at first but gradually gaining momentum as word spread. Car boots were filled with bottles for the elderly, ladies' shopping trolleys and baby buggies were loaded up, and youngsters carried water to the housebound. No sooner had the two-hour session finished than another larger lorry load arrived and the chain-gang got back to work. By the end arms and backs ached, but we all had water.

Molly Walker
Stroud Shambles WI

I was the only person using the showers at Stroud Leisure Centre when I heard two people come in followed by heavy sighs, delighted moaning, and cries of 'Oh! Wonderful!' What was I missing? The 'refugees' emerged as I was dressing. They had come from Gloucester and it was their first shower for seven days. No wonder they were so ecstatic!

A notice hung on a bowser in Eastcombe. Springs in the village were used by residents when the taps dried up. (E. Crouch)

Siân Callen
Woodchester WI

I was staying in Painswick during the week after the flash flooding. The cottage wasn't flooded but our mains water eventually dried up, although fortunately there is a crystal clear stream across the lane. Every morning and afternoon I met locals filling watering cans, bowls, plastic milk bottles, every sort of container at the well, but it was the concern and practical assistance for those who needed help that impressed me most. And of course the humour: 'Water? We've got plenty! It's just not in the tap.'

Edna Helson
Leonard Stanley WI

We were the lucky ones! Only twenty hours without running water caused by a burst pipe. It was long enough to make me appreciate the luxury of flowing water in constant supply and hit home the hardships and desolation of those without water for much of their lives.

Every available type of tanker was used to keep the bowsers filled with water.
(Mary Howl)

Diana Wall

Avening WI

Gradually, the picture unfolded for those of us over 700ft above sea level – kept informed by local radio and television. It could have been a different country – pictures of Mythe Waterworks flooded, the efforts to protect Walham Switching Station and the waters creeping higher in Tewkesbury and Gloucester.

I am Clerk to Minchinhampton Parish Council, and Stroud District Council kept us informed by e-mail, so, as the water supply progressively failed, we were able to advise parishioners. 'If the water goes off, where do I get it for my stock?' (The NFU had this one covered.) 'Do we get our supply from Black Gutter?' (Yes, the spring that feeds Chalford pumping station and the reservoir on the common.) 'Do I need to go to Sainsbury's to get bottled water?' (No, it will be available free.)

Minchinhampton, Avening and Cherington all had water. Sons returned home – I thought I'd seen the last of piles of washing and the shower room looking like a bomb had hit it! I offered my bathroom or washing machine to friends in Gloucester.

> **IMPORTANT**
>
> **Health and Safety Advice**
>
> **When water supply returns through taps**
>
> - **Do NOT** drink the water even after boiling it!
>
> - **Do NOT** use the water for food preparation or washing dishes!
>
> - **Do NOT** use the water for ice making!
>
> - **Do NOT** use for cleaning your teeth!
>
> - **Do NOT** use for making baby feeds!
>
> The water **CAN** be used for flushing toilets, bathing and showering.
>
> **Bottled water** or **boiled bowser water** remains the **only safe** source of drinking water until further notice.
>
> ♦ ♦ Make sure that ALL taps are turned off – to help fill the network more quickly
> ♦ ♦ As the supply is temporary, tap water may be intermittent & may be discoloured
> ♦ ♦ You will be informed when the tap water is safe to drink
>
> **Electricity**
>
> Your electricity supply may need checking if you have been flooded. Please call the Central Networks emergency help line on 0800 096 1194
>
> Do NOT use any mains powered electrical appliances that have been in contact with water until advised that a registered electrician has checked them.
>
> Do NOT go near any exposed wiring, as it may still be live.
>
> Do NOT attempt any electrical repairs or connection of temporary supplies yourself - always use a registered electrician.

Warning notices were issued to households when water started to flow back through taps.

Sue Makin

Woodmancote WI

Our village hall was a water depot. On the first Tuesday I heard water was being delivered so went round to help, and that was it! I spent most of that week at the hall heaving packs of water about or giving it away. We received anything from two to five pallets on a daily basis over the next two weeks, and the words 'form a chain' will stay in my memory for some time; one chain passed the packs of water through the windows into the small hall, and another chain collected and stacked.

We all learnt how heavy water is, especially packs of 6×2 litres. Much gossip ensued between helpers and those fetching water and the three most frequently

Once the tap water was back on, the bowsers were collected together at Staverton Airport.
(Pete Wilson)

Lorries came from all over the country to pick up the bowsers.
(Pete Wilson)

asked questions were 'Where do you live?', 'How long have you lived there?' and 'Oh, so you must know so and so?' I've lived in the village for nearly thirty years and met people who have lived in the village equally as long, whom I've never met before! The lack of water was an inconvenience and hard work, but enjoyable.

chapter eight

HELPING

Dennis Lyes, husband of Gill Lyes
Horsbere WI

A large number of residents in Longlevens had already suffered serious flooding as a result of storms just a couple of weeks earlier and were just about coming to terms with their situation. This second bout of flooding was the worst this area has ever seen. Particularly bad were the Cypress Gardens, Clomoney Way and Park Avenue areas, which had been inundated by water overflowing from the Horsbere Brook, some of the water becoming contaminated with sewage. Floodwater also engulfed parts of the Manor Park, Cheltenham Road, Plock Court and Longford Lane areas. River water coming down the Severn and the Avon added to the problem.

Electricity supplies failed on Sunday night making residents resort to candles and torches, and battery radios to keep in touch with the outside world. Water supplies also ceased as reservoir capacities dwindled to zero after the water treatment works at Tewkesbury closed down.

Holy Trinity Church Hall was opened and a generator unit hastily found, providing power for moderate lighting while gas appliances provided cooking facilities. Word spread that the hall was open to provide food, drink and shelter for those in serious need and volunteers were sought to assist in whatever capacity they could.

Slowly a system began to evolve. Bottled water was obtained from willing supermarkets and ultimately from the Red Cross and Severn Trent. A few volunteers began to formulate a parish-wide calling system to identify those people in need. Water and hot food began to be delivered where required and a rota system was set up in the kitchen for volunteer staff. Power returned overnight on Monday, which alleviated the predicament a little.

Water delivery began with volunteer drivers and assistants on daily rounds. Callers at the hall were welcome to a drink and a sandwich and helpful information was made available.

The return of water to the taps on 3 August, although it had to be boiled, began to reduce the demand for water and on 6 August, when the water was declared fit to drink, the system was shut down and the hall closed.

Daily life returned to normal for most people, but not for those who were flooded: their struggle will continue for months. They live in dread of more flooding, but know that the community has learnt a great deal from coping with such a situation and could quickly spring into action again if needed.

Irene Jones
Horsbere WI

Some of our members offered to help with manning an emergency kitchen at Holy Trinity Church Hall and checking on those who weren't able to get to bowsers or obtain bottled water. I was preparing for my imminent holiday in Canada, but felt compelled to volunteer too, and arrived at the church hall on Friday 27 July to help in the kitchen.

Despite the seriousness of the situation, there was an air of excitement around the hall as we were told to expect HRH Princess Anne, who was visiting Longlevens. She arrived around 1 p.m. and without hesitation walked straight into the kitchen, eager to know details of what we were doing to help the flood victims. She commented on the ample supply of tea, coffee, sandwiches and cakes – plus the emergency stocks of tins and packets of food, most of which had been given by local people anxious to help. The princess spent about half an hour with us, but only managed to drink half her cup of coffee as she was so eager to talk to all the volunteers and to show her very genuine sympathy for those so badly affected by the floods. What a great lady – no fuss, no grand entrance – just a purposeful and personal interest and concern for the people whose homes and lives had been wrecked by this freak weather.

The Bishop of Tewkesbury (right) visiting Deerhurst. (David Bowers)

Velma Sutton

Apperley & Deerhurst WI

The community spirit in Apperley has been reinforced. We've been welcomed in by complete strangers and become good friends. Others have helped with laundry and cooking meals. Two experienced campers in the village spent a morning levelling up the caravan, which is to be our home until the cottage is repaired. An 88-year-old lady who's lived in the village all her life said, 'Your house never floods'. Well now we know better!

Marion Gilliland

Kemble & Ewen WI

A nurse living in Cirencester and working at Cheltenham General Hospital volunteered to take Thames tap water for her colleagues to drink. People had religiously washed, squashed and recycled most of their plastic bottles, so she had to make SOS phone calls to friends to find enough bottles to fill her car boot with water.

Anne Turner

Ashleworth & Hasfield WI

I was invited to send two groups of residents who'd been flooded or helped in the aftermath to tour the gardens at Highgrove. A gentleman who'd been rescued by helicopter went. Another couple had 5ft of water through their house. Someone else was flooded and had to wade through water at armpit level to rescue belongings. One man delivered water to forty-seven houses each day, to the elderly or large families. Another gave out water for fifteen days in the village hall and, when it was too heavy, carried it to homes in his car. Our local vicar also went, as his moral support was invaluable.

We arrived at Highgrove at 1.20 p.m. and after security checks headed for the Orchard Room, walking through a disinfectant dip first, as the threat of foot and mouth disease was in everyone's mind.

Like everyone's garden, everywhere looked green and lush. The gardeners were busy trying to catch up with work delayed by the weather. After the tour we had a welcome cup of tea and visited the shop. The visit had been an excellent tonic after the recent problems.

Julie Hayes

Gretton WI

Gretton was cut off by Friday afternoon, as the main road and Gretton Fields were both impassable by cars. The water was running through the Bugatti pub off the hill behind the village. The owners of the houses opposite don't know who the young people were who stopped and helped put up barriers and bail out, but they worked for at least three hours before moving on.

On Saturday morning another young couple knocked on one of their doors to ask if they could use the toilet. They had to leave the motorway the night before, saw the Bugatti car park was up a slope, so had spent the night there in their car. The owner of the house wished they'd knocked earlier, as he had a spare room, but he let them use his bathroom and gave them breakfast.

Water rushing down the hill by the Bugatti pub in Gretton.
(Julie Hayes)

Verna Boughton

Hardwicke WI

Twice I tried to phone two elderly friends to see if they were okay. They were out to lunch. At 4.20 p.m. they called me. 'Can you help? We're flooded right through and don't know what to do.' I phoned Stroud District Council for advice. The receptionist suggested ringing 999 but Gloucestershire Fire Brigade were so busy that after ten minutes I was put through to Wiltshire. Good advice was given but no help was available.

My husband and I drove over to our friends and immediately switched off the electricity supply. With help from others we managed to get small items of furniture upstairs. The small freezer was floating in the kitchen, as was the vinyl floor covering. The dog's bed was floating as she stood up to her tummy in floodwater, looking frightened. We did all we could – paddling in over eight inches of cold, dirty water. Then we took our friends and their dog safely back to our house. By this time poor Tom, 86 and suffering from Alzheimer's, didn't know where he was or what was happening. It was very distressing for us all. We quickly changed the beds around. Brandy the dog was the only one who slept that night.

In the morning we went back to their lovely old thatched, chocolate-box cottage. The flood had receded a little but the garden was still deeply under water with goldfish swimming round and a kingfisher who thought it was Christmas! We evacuated more furniture upstairs. Suddenly the water in the house went down, but the smell was unbelievable and indescribable! We emptied the fridge and freezer – all waterlogged – and started to pull up carpets, vinyl, rugs etc.

My husband and I were both running out of steam – so in true WI spirit I decided to go looking for some strong men. I found them! A delightful, young, strong Frenchman and a coalman used to hard work. They got the flooring up and struggled to get it all outside. Another neighbour knew a young electrician who came out from Tuffley – on a Sunday – and wouldn't hear of charging. He tested and got back the essential electrics. Another brought a de-humidifier which has worked overtime ever since.

Monday – another crisis – we woke to no electric and no water. The electricity was only off for two and a half hours, but the water was off for over two weeks. Our friends stayed with us for a week – they're now in a caravan in their picturesque garden. Will they be back in their lovely old home in six months time? Who knows?

Chic Dempster, husband of Chris Dempster

Moreton-in-Marsh WI

At around 11 a.m. I had a call from the Redesdale Hall Management Committee, asking if I could go to the Town Hall and organise shelter for people in distress.

Moreton-in-Marsh railway station looking more like a canal.
(Chic Dempster)

I couldn't walk directly there and had to make my way from Budgens via the rail station, where the water was not so deep, and down Oxford Street. The manager of the Tesco shop by the hall immediately donated tea and coffee. Local residents brought beds, blankets, dry socks and food. Three people who helped were stranded themselves; it was wonderful to see how people pulled together. We looked after around fifty people, some of whom slept on the upper floor that night. I returned to the hall at about 7 a.m. the following morning. The flood had receded and traffic was starting to move, but many people had to start coming to terms with destroyed homes, businesses and vehicles.

June Flude

Newtown WI

Eight of our members here in Tewkesbury were flooded; one lives in a bungalow, so lost an awful lot more than those in houses.

Once villagers in Amesbury in Wiltshire heard their local WI was collecting things to help us, they all wanted to help. A few shops donated goods or gave a discount on items they bought. Then two WI committee members drove to my house with a van full of what they had accumulated. There were duvets and covers, blankets, sheets, pillows, bolts of nets, cushions, tablecloths, tea-towels, toys, boxes of cleaning materials, the list goes on. Our members have taken what they need to help them until they can return to their renovated homes and the rest we are taking to the Salvation Army. Their kindness, and the thought that went into the range of items collected, overwhelmed us.

Flooded members from Newtown WI in Tewkesbury receiving items collected by Amesbury WI in Wiltshire. (June Flude)

Pat Cobley
Norton WI

Most houses and farms in Priors Norton are on the hill topped by St Mary's, the disappearing church. Two houses on the A38 and one at the bottom of Marlpit Lane were flooded. The floods cut us off for almost a week, the electricity was off for a short while and tap water went when the River Severn flooded.

A local farmer with a big tractor brought bottled water left at the King's Head. We never got a bowser; washing and flushing were done with rainwater from garden butts. The tractor also took a local GP living on the hill to his car at the King's Head, so he could get to patients. By 26 July the flood was going down and 4-wheel drive cars could get out. A lorry brought more drinking water and the milkman arrived. On Friday the 27th the road and the dips at the bottom of our lanes were passable, so I went food shopping.

During the flood, we went out in our wellies via the footpath at the back of the hill, coming out at the clay pigeon shooting club on the main road. People who had pets at the kennels in Church Lane left or collected their pets at this point.

*The only way
out of Sandhurst
for some was
by boat or in
a tractor.*
(Alan Moore)

Joan Cook

Phoenix WI

Here in Cirencester the heavy rain affected roads and many people's homes and businesses. At the Pop-In, where my friend Sylvia and I work as volunteers each Monday at the Housebound Club, the water damage was horrendous. It was unsafe to enter the premises for a week, during which time walls, cupboards, linen – everything – was waterlogged with mildew everywhere. We spent ages cleaning everything, helping to get the centre reopened.

*Janet and Tony
Anderson from
Sandhurst dressed to do
battle with the waist-
high floodwater.
They were saved the
experience by a
neighbour who collected
their provisions on his
motorbike.* (Ann David)

Sandhurst WI members and their husbands prepare to join a protest march in Tewkesbury against building on floodplains. (Alan Moore)

Water from Quay Street in Gloucester being pumped into the River Severn after the river level receded. (Joan Heath)

Elizabeth James

The Shires WI

On Sunday, Shire Hall was evacuated due to the rising river and flooding around the Quay. The Emergency Management Service, which had been operating since Friday, was evacuated to the Tri Service Centre at Waterwells in Quedgeley. As my manager is part of the Welfare Team, I was asked to provide admin support from Tuesday, once the back-up IT system had been set up. There was a bank of PCs on the ground floor and servers in a van outside and the team were based on the second floor, so it provided useful body magic constantly using the stairs.

For the first two days I travelled to and from work via the M50 and M5: 178 miles and five hours travelling. Everyone involved in the Emergency Management Service worked incredibly hard for long hours trying to overcome innumerable issues that arose.

Angela Danby

Tibberton & Taynton WI

When I lost my mother recently I never thought a few weeks later the annexe she lived in would bring help to a fellow member. Di and her husband Roy, no strangers to flooding, were inundated with over 2ft of water. They contemplated moving into a caravan or camping upstairs. Coming to terms with the loss of my mother and feeling lost in the house we shared for ten years, Di and Roy accepting my offer to stay in the annexe, along with their collie dog, has proved a tremendous help to both parties.

Daisy Sowman

Winchcombe WI

Twenty-three people were stranded in Winchcombe at St Peter's Centre. Our Youth Minister phoned around to find people willing to take them in. He rang me at 10.20 p.m. and I offered a double bed to a lovely couple from Bath. They were travelling to Redditch to visit their daughter.

The motorway closed and they left it at Cheltenham, making their way to Winchcombe. After tea and biscuits they went to bed and left in the morning at 5.15 a.m. with many thanks and a donation to St Peter's Centre. I later received a vase of flowers and a note to say they arrived safely at their destination.

Sue Wilson

Twyver WI

I worked at BBC Radio Gloucestershire for some years, so when I heard on Sunday that many of us would be losing our water supply, I knew listeners would be phoning the radio station for information and offered to help. My husband was already there and, along with others, we took calls until 2 a.m. and then spent long days over the next week answering calls.

Press conferences with Gold Command were broadcast daily and the experts frequently quizzed on air for answers to listeners' worries. The queries and the mood of callers changed daily. At first, the elderly and disabled were worried about how they would get water, then listeners rang to report empty bowsers or where they were needed; we passed that information to Severn Trent. 'Where is bottled water being delivered today?' 'What should we do with the empty bottles?'

We could also offer people individual help. We collated lists of emergency numbers, found portaloos for a wedding and volunteers to take water to farm animals, and advised on which roads to take to avoid flooded areas. Water came back on but wasn't drinkable; mothers wanted advice on washing baby clothes and at what temperature to wash. One man wanted to know if it was safe to change the water in his goldfish bowl! We took a steady stream of around 100 calls an hour for several days.

By the end of the week all the radio staff were exhausted. Some of them had not been home for several days because they too had been cut off by the floods, but it was good to know we were able to do something to help.

chapter nine

AFTERMATH

Annette Grafton

Bibury & Barnsley WI

Saturday 21 July: Kitchen and garage flooded and main drain blocked. Kind friends bailed and swept but the water kept rising. Dared not use any water for fear of back up from foul water. Overwhelming offers of baths, showers, lavatories, meals etc. More friends carried small furniture upstairs and large pieces to the village hall in case the river broke its bank. High water deadline came and went without that happening. I used the village hall facilities.

Sunday 22nd: Hectic morning pumping, somewhat revived by gin and tonics all round. Three large firemen arrived but would not pump out the water as nowhere to put it and hurried away after placing more sandbags.

Tuesday 24th: The vicar spent the whole afternoon sweeping and bailing out the water. All this, of course, is only the beginning. It will be off with the plaster, up with the tiled floor, out with the units. Everything must go.

Jean Tebbett
Central Cheltenham WI

Two weeks after the flood we went on a river cruise on the Avon from Evesham. The river was back to normal and had been opened again. The owner of the boat had lost his bigger boat, which ended up with a lamp-post through its hull. It was a lovely afternoon and we enjoyed a cream tea, but there were signs of devastation along the river; people's belongings festooned in trees, smashed up caravans and sunken ones in the river, some houses completely written off, the water having risen 22ft.

The devastation left behind at the weir bridge at Abbey Mill on the Avon in Tewkesbury.
(Philippa Keen)

Just one of many boats that sunk at their moorings on the Avon at Tewkesbury. (Matilda Pearce)

*More devastated boats
at Tewkesbury.*
(Philippa Keen)

Janice Cole

Woodmancote WI

I little realised as I left my part-time job at Leisure@Cheltenham on Friday
that I wouldn't be back there for possibly a year. I didn't manage to get
home to Woodmancote until the following morning and hadn't realised
how badly the leisure centre had been hit. I later learned that, at about
teatime on Friday, water started to trickle in, soon becoming a torrent and
forcing a speedy evacuation as the water reached waist height. The lake
and pool became one. Contaminated water had got into the plant room and
fish were happily exercising in the centre. The wooden floors buckled, one

*Everything had to be
pressure hosed and
sanitised, even the
garden furniture at
the Coal House
pub in Apperley
where floods were
a foot deep.*
(Rose Williams)

*The devastation left by the
flood inside the Coal House
pub. Oil from the deep fat
fryers floated on top of the
water making matters worse.*
(Rose Williams)

set of doors still cannot be opened as the floor has risen by 2ft. The computers are 'kaput' and all my work was lost. We were deployed to distribute bottled water and then told to wait for the centre to re-open. As I write this I am still being paid for doing nothing, but I am sure that will soon change!

Jeanette Aldred

Bredon WI

Friday 20 July: Holidaying on the Isle of Man. My son called to say my home may be flooded. I rang a friend who went round to have a look. She called later to say water was cascading down the road. There was between 4 and 6in in my house and the garden was like a lake.

Saturday 21st: Both sons rang to say everyone had problems getting home and one of them spent the night in Twyning. His girlfriend was stranded in Evesham. My 93-year-old Dad was staying in a care home in Worcester. I spent most of the day trying to track him down and finally found out the care home had been flooded and he'd been taken to Malvern.

Sunday 22nd: My son called. They'd managed to get to our house. The car was on a pile of stones because of the force of the water running through the road. He tried to rescue pot plants and spent the day sweeping up and drying out all my paperwork. Water poured out of everything. It was in the cupboards but had receded from the carpets. The curtains were soaked, also the new settee and chairs. I called my Dad and spoke to him. He had been sick and was looking forward to seeing us – I just wanted to get home.

Tuesday 24th: We caught the early ferry and a friend called to say there was no tap water. We filled up our tank in the camper van and got supplies. We arrived home late and checked Dad's property across the road and then squelched around our house, sleeping in the camper van, exhausted.

Wednesday 25th: We started to realise the full extent of the damage. I had recently bought a 'Bed in a Bag' set and it was full of water. All my bags in a cupboard in the cloakroom were soaked, and my briefcase and all my schoolwork and reports were completely ruined. We rang the insurers and worked all day trying to dry out important papers – birth certificates, marriage certificate, etc. At least the ink had not run, so we were still legal! A friend came to help cut up carpets and we worked until 11 p.m. dragging them outside.

Thursday 26th: We waited and waited for the loss adjuster and my husband went to collect Dad from the care home. I prepared his home and then continued pouring water out of everything and trying to dry things out. Dad was traumatised. The loss adjuster arrived. There would be three different agencies coming to assess the damage and we could move into a hotel or rented property, but we couldn't leave my Dad so decided to live in our camper van.

Friday 27th: Spent the day looking after Dad and clearing up. I went to Bredon Church as I was on the flower rota.

Monday 30th: The council came to collect our carpets and we watched a machine eat the new three-piece suite.

Saturday 4 August: The 'Disaster Man' came and said the cork tiles needed lifting – we had tried but found them very difficult. He assured us someone would come, but no one did.

Monday 6th: My husband started chiselling up tiles and took them to the tip. There seemed to be hundreds.

Friday 10th: A building surveyor said everything would have to be ripped out – kitchen units, skirting boards, doorframes and doors which didn't fit any more, and the plasterboard would have to come off the walls. We felt devastated.

Sunday 12th: I noticed black mould on my pine Welsh dresser so we took everything off it and looked underneath. There were thick hairy lumps of mould over everything. We spent all afternoon and evening scraping them off and scrubbing with bleach, feeling absolutely dreadful. We went to Cheltenham to buy de-bugging spray, but didn't find any. We felt desolate.

Monday 13th: I rang the insurance company at 6.45 a.m. as I had been awake all night. Something had to be done to help us. We just had people coming and taking photographs and measuring up. At 10 a.m. a white van arrived and two men whizzed round tearing out the skirting boards and the fireplace and dumping everything on our front drive. They sprayed the floor and got me to sign something to say the carpets, underlay and cork tiles had been removed. I objected, as we had done all this, but they insisted and left us one de-humidifier and a blower for four rooms. Later, the insurers called to see if the workmen had been and said someone would come back in another week.

Tuesday 21st: Here we are one week later and over a month since the floods. Nothing has happened, except we are living with the noise and heat of the blower and de-humidifier every day and alternating between despair and thinking we're coping. It's now 7 p.m. and again I have been waiting all day for the 'Disaster Man'. He says he is coming, but he hasn't yet. . . .

Anne Turner

Ashleworth & Hasfield WI

I visited Ashleworth Church today. It had been cleaned but was empty of furniture. The organ is on a high plinth but the water reached up to the pedals.

The pulpit at Tirley Church was toppled by the force of the floodwater. (Tony Price)

Tirley churchyard, showing the high water marks on the trees. The gate was found a few hundred yards down the road. (Tony Price)

It now awaits repair. The force of the water pushed the pews into a large pile in the middle of the church. Some were damaged and all have gone for repair or replacement. It was so sad to see.

Later I went into Tirley Church, which is in an even worse state. The floodwater ripped the pews from their fittings on the wall and pulled the plaster off. The pulpit fell over and now has a diagonal line from top to bottom. One side is still brown but the other side, which was in the water, is bleached white. Goodness knows what pollutants caused this effect. The whole church looks derelict.

It will be a long time before both churches are back in use.

Jen Poole
Coaley WI

Shopping locally I met a pleasant lady anxious to buy some nightwear. She explained she was a 'refugee'. I sympathised with her but was unable to detect any foreign accent. She then put me right: 'I'm a refugee from Cheltenham. I've come to live with my daughter until my home is safe and power and water restored.'

Two neighbours offered daily 'showering and laundry facilities' to relatives. Many containers were filled with Coaley tap water, as bottled water doesn't make a decent cup of tea!

Joan Heath
Hempsted WI

In an effort to prevent Castlemeads power station from flooding, a pipe was laid along the bypass as far as Llanthony Bridge, so water could be pumped into the canal. My husband was assessing the situation in Sudmeadow Road, which had suffered badly from flooding. The only way to reach Sudmeadow from our house in Hempsted was by a very convoluted route around Gloucester. When he returned to his car in Llanthony Road, the pipe had reached the bridge, which was closed. The only way home was on foot, through the flood in Hempsted Lane. The car remained in Llanthony Road for three days!

Ella Hardman
Sedgeberrow WI

Our end of the village is still a bit like a ghost town as several families had to move out while everything is removed from their homes. They say that it could

The River Severn came within inches of closing the Castlemeads substation in Gloucester, seen here in the foreground with the quay and the prison at the top. (Jennie Moss)

The armed forces and fire crews worked tirelessly to save the substation. They laid pipes to divert the water into Gloucester Docks. (Brian Govier)

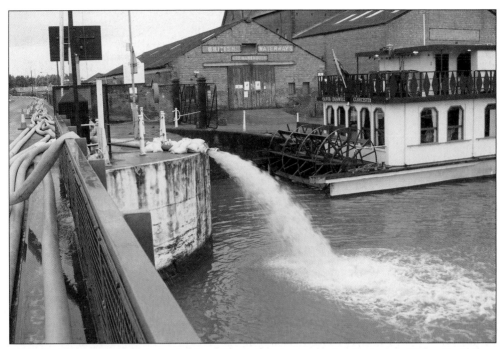

Water had been drained from the canal and the dock basin to take the piped water. (Brian Govier)

be six to nine months before people will be able to go back. Caravans and mobile homes are now appearing, as people want to be near to their houses. Two of our friends are living in a two-berth caravan on their drive, but hope to rent a cottage for the winter. Our next-door neighbours are in a hotel, but hope to move soon to a mobile home on their drive.

Diana Le Clair

Central Cheltenham WI

It was weird going into shops to find shelves empty because delivery lorries were unable to get through, or from panic buying, or to be told certain items were strictly one-per-customer (wet-wipes, dry shampoo, long-life milk, floor/surface/toilet cleaning wipes, anti-bacterial handwash, etc.). I even heard underpants were sold out! Neighbours have been checking that we're alright, several friends have phoned, and Meals on Wheels thoughtfully brought bottled water with Mummy's lunch. People are talking to strangers in shops and helping one another to find alternative things to use – everyone has a tale to tell.

Many roads were left badly damaged, like Castle Street in Winchcombe. (Alan Herod)

Floods on the Ledbury road near Dymock left this bridge over the River Leadon badly damaged. (Ruth Clowes)

Vi Banks

Longlevens WI

After the flood, the water and electricity were cut off. I think it was then that the realisation came that this was a disaster. If it hadn't been for the armed forces we would certainly have been without electricity for a long time. We owe them a debt of gratitude for saving the power station.

My husband is 91 and I am 87. The voluntary people at the church hall distribution centre were marvellous. They called every day to see if we wanted bowser or drinking water. As a result we have met Reg, one of the volunteers, who said he would help us in any way he could and since then has been true to his word.

I have since been to see a WI member who was flooded. She still has driers in the house. The noise was terrific. She said she just sat and cried; the tasks seemed so enormous. It made me realise how lucky we had been. Another few inches and we would have been in her situation.

The biggest problem was making sure my husband did not drink the bowser water. I am sure that mothers had the same problem with their children.

Devastation at Painswick. (Maggie Drake)

Glenda Ford
Tibberton & Taynton WI

I manage the refectory at Tewkesbury Abbey. By lunchtime on Friday 20 July it had been raining like stair-rods for seven hours. There was no one about and the road was beginning to flood. I decided to shut and send my staff home. They all lived in Tewkesbury.

After seven hours trying to get home to Tibberton and a trip on a tractor, I spent the night on the phone telling Abbey staff where to find food. They had set up a refuge for stranded motorists. A coach of thirty-five elderly people had been on a daytrip and none of them had any medication with them. Caravaners going on holiday were diverted off the M5 as it was blocked and ended up spending several days stranded in Tewkesbury, at the centre of one of the biggest ever peace time rescue operations.

The vicar and parishioners spent several worrying days making sandbags to prevent water getting in. It wasn't completely successful and for the first time in 200 years there was water inside the Abbey. The cellar also flooded with a massive loss of food stock, three new freezers and fridges, Flower Guild equipment and priceless Christmas figures.

Sandbags at the doors of Tewkesbury Abbey. (Matilda Pearce)

Furniture and belongings in the street in Tewkesbury. The road had become part of the river.
(Matilda Pearce)

It was like coming home when we got back to the Abbey ten days later; all around the town everyone was helping each other. As you drove through the streets all you saw was wet carpets, wet furniture. People's lives were in ruins and they faced months of drying out and repairs. My staff spent the first day back getting Red Cross parcels to people and we fed exhausted fire crews who were pumping out houses and businesses, desperately trying to support people.

It's been a very strange month. It should have been our busy time, but it's been, and will continue to be, a very hard struggle to rebuild the business. For some there will be more lasting trauma and some businesses may never reopen.